Dear Linda,

Make Wishes!

Lee Ravine

RIDING SOLO

MY JOURNEY THROUGH LOVE AND MADNESS

LEE B. RAVINE B.A., M.S.

TRIMARK PRESS, INC.
DEERFIELD BEACH, FLORIDA

This memoir was complied from the author's journal entries. Some names have been changed and situations altered to protect privacy.

REQUEST FOR PERMISSION TO MAKE COPIES OF ANY PART OF THE WORK SHOULD BE MAILED TO THE FOLLOWING ADDRESS: PERMISSION DEPARTMENT, TriMark Press, Inc., 368 SOUTH MILITARY TRAIL, DEERFIELD BEACH, FLORIDA 33442 800-889-0693 / WWW.TriMarkPress.com

LIBRARY OF CONGRESS CATALOGING-IN-PUBLICATIONS DATA IS AVAILABLE

RAVINE, LEE B.

RIDING SOLO: MY JOURNEY THROUGH LOVE AND MADNESS

1. PSYCHOLOGY   2. PSYCHOLOGY STUDY   3. MENTAL ILLNESS

4. CAREGIVER   5. CO-DEPENDENCY   6. DOMESTIC ABUSE   7. SELF-HELP

ISBN: 978-0-9829702-0-1

L10, FIRST EDITION

PRINTED IN THE UNITED STATES

COVER PHOTO BY: RICHARD ELKINS PHOTOGRAPHY
WWW.RICHELKINS.COM

*This book is dedicated to the memory of
my mother and father, Steve Z., Mindy and Bill.*

CONTENTS

FOREWORD

When looking upon the white blanket of a newly fallen snow, I am often reminded of an elementary school science lesson, "Each snowflake is unique and individual."

In my three decades as a couples' counselor, I have seen uniqueness in the individuals sitting in my office. Each husband and wife both mirror and diverge from other partnered couples. The variations create an infinite number of unique combinations.

When Bob and Lee first came into my office, they seemed at first blush a typical couple. The initial blanket of snow was calm. Our work together would soon disabuse me of that notion.

Lee has written a moving story of life's journey. It includes the years and sessions the three of us worked together. Bob's "uniquenes" made the counseling more difficult and her ensuing life with him a challenge. The process she describes is both an interesting and emotionally gripping story. The reader can empathize with the characters' similarities to people and events in their own lives.

I feel honored for having been a part of this journey. Lee's growth, progress and graduation from the school of hard knocks denotes a sense of satisfaction. It is these types of "snowflakes" and the guidance I have hopefully provided that make psychotherapy rewarding.

Ben Adler, Ph.D.

ACKNOWLEDGMENTS

For your words of encouragement my thanks to Chuck Sambuchino, Emily Rosen, Bob Davis, Doreen Stiller, Marty and Lynn Weisberg, Space Coast Writer's Guild, and South Florida Writer's Organization.

I would like to give special thanks to the following people:

- My loving family and friends,

- Ben Adler, Ph.D., without whom I would never have survived my journey,

- Holly Katz, Ph.D., Director of Programs and Services —Center for Group Counseling,

- Adam Friedman, Ph.D.,

- My talented Editor, John Johnson, and

- My equally talented Vice President/Marketing at TriMark Press; Elizabeth Hickman.

PART ONE

THE RIDE
BEGINS

CHAPTER ONE

In 1959, if anyone would have told me 15 years down the road I would be a 35-year old divorcee with an adolescent child, and about to enter the singles' world for a second time, I would have regarded that person as nuts.

Thoughts about reentering the singles' scene filled me with trepidation, followed by remembering that I already hated the ritual:

1. Applying war-paint.
2. Dressing provocatively.
3. Making small-talk with perverts, trolls and an endless parade of married men cheating on wives.

And within that social minefield, I would also be forced to struggle with the same self-doubt that haunted me as a teenager—how do I look? What should I say? Will he like me? And that soon followed by never being sure how to respond to the one question I dreaded the most: "Why did your marriage fail?"

I didn't feel like a failure; I was just tired of beating a dead horse.

However, nothing prepared me for the world turning upside down following my hand rubber-stamped entrance to a single-parents' dance, and a familiar voice calling out as I entered the dimly lit ballroom.

"Hey Lee! Come on over here. I want to introduce you to someone."

After my eyes adjusted to the subdued lighting, I recognized Beth, the hostess responsible for making sure everyone mingled.

Beth directed her attention to the attractive man standing beside her, while shielding her mouth behind a hand.

"Would you like me to introduce you to a nice lady?" she whispered toward him.

"No!" the man replied in a booming voice.

Beth and I shrugged and stared at each other in disbelief. I felt more embarrassed for her than for myself. The man didn't look like a jerk; he was neatly dressed and well groomed.

If he wanted to be left alone, then what's he doing at a dance Ms. Freud wondered?

In truth, and in an effort to shore up self-esteem, I found it difficult to understand why he would reject this lovely creature standing before him. At that moment I felt confident about my appearance, even blowing a kiss to my reflection in a full-length mirror before leaving home.

After a couple of regulars asked me to dance, and I joined a group of women for a disco set, I felt it was time for a break. I headed toward the unoccupied chairs lining the ballroom's perimeter. Sitting in an isolated corner I noticed the cute guy with whom Beth had attempted the introduction.

I'm not sure what drew me to him—curiosity or chemistry? Given what had happened earlier, I apparently didn't think much of the aphorism: "Let sleeping dogs lie."

As I approached, Mr. Rudely Cute appeared to be in a trance. His face was devoid of expression and I considered the possibility that he may be depressed. It was obvious he needed to talk with Ms. Freud.

His face lit-up after I inquired if the seat next to him was available; he motioned for me to sit.

Was this the same person I had encountered earlier, Ms. Freud queried? How could he have changed so dramatically from one moment to the next?

Little did I know I would be asking myself these questions many, many times in the years to come—but it didn't begin that way.

After introductions, Bob apologized for being abrupt earlier. The throbbing background music made conversation difficult and we agreed to meet a little later at a nearby diner.

Predictably, the diner talk later focused on life events leading up to being at the dance:

Bob had been divorced two years and was the father of an 18-month-old son, who in turn lived in Florida with the ex-wife; I hungered for a loving, stable relationship. I was the product of divorced parents, and out on my own at age 16. Shortly thereafter, I entered into a marriage with an older man who had difficulty expressing emotion, and who should have remained a bachelor.

Small talk ensued, followed by mutually agreeing it wouldn't be fair to disappoint our already known New Year's Eve dates. Our conversation concluded with an agreement to wait until after January 1 before seeing one another again.

Known to me even before he left, Bob definitely made an impression. He was charming, witty, intelligent, good looking—and that beguiling barometer of sexual attraction was near the top of the scale. The clincher was when he drove out of the parking lot in a brand new, white, Cadillac El Dorado.

Has your knight finally arrived, asked Ms. Freud?

Thinking about the evening made me giddy. I had difficulty falling asleep. But after the euphoria, something Bob had said began to gnaw at me. The year of his divorce and the age of his son did not jibe.

Ms. Freud queried: What man leaves a pregnant wife?

There appeared to be a chink in my knight's armor.

More attention to details, cautioned Ms. Freud.

The next day a single red rose and a romantic note were at my front door.

"A promise of things to come," said the note.

The birth/divorce time line that concerned me the night before seemed less important to Ms. Freud and me in the light of day. Somebody was paying attention to me for the first time in years.

That was all I cared about.

CHAPTER TWO

Each date thereafter with Bob was perfectly planned and executed—including money freely spent. Likewise, his prowess in the bedroom was exhilarating, leading me to heights of ecstasy I never knew existed.

However, after several months I suspected something was weighing heavily on him. Gone was the fun-loving, talkative, affectionate person with whom I had fallen in love.

When I inquired, he assured me everything was fine. But it was clear something was wrong and he was having difficulty articulating it. That was until one night he blurted, "I have something to tell you, but I'm afraid you'll get angry and won't see me anymore."

What could possibly be so terrible, wondered Ms. Freud?

Then I remembered something Bob revealed early in our relationship. He had been living with his mother ever since his last girlfriend packed his belongings in shopping bags and placed them on her porch. I often wondered if there was more to the story. What was bothering him might be a dark secret from before his girlfriend threw him out.

I assured him there were only two things I would find unforgivable: "One is if you're an ax-murderer and the other is if you're a child molester," I said, half-joking.

"No, no, that's not it. I lied to you about my wife and child. I made up the whole story. I've never been married. I used my nephew's birth certificate to join the parent's organization."

Ms. Freud queried: This was what he didn't want to say?

I smiled, and Bob responded with a hug, quickly confident his confession would not affect our relationship.

Bob had asked me to marry him shortly after we began dating, and eventually I met his family. His mother, Bea, was an attractive, vivacious, flirtatious, widow who talked, cleaned and shopped obsessively. And the moment I met them, I liked Bob's brother Allan, wife Jackie and precocious children.

However, I was not ready to make a commitment of any kind. I had been divorced less than a year and I felt my daughter Michelle required my full attention. Whomever I married would have to understand that Michelle and I were a "package deal." I did not want any more children and I made it clear that if this was an issue Bob would either have to come to terms with it, or move on.

When I didn't immediately agree to his marriage proposal, Bob surprised me by loudly proclaiming, "If you don't make a commitment I will disappear off the face of the earth."

At first I thought he was joking; I also felt our relationship was moving too fast. I suggested what I thought was a viable plan where we would see each other once during the week and every other weekend, when Michelle was at her father's house.

Bob's pinched expression confirmed that he meant what he said. And although I resented the pressure to make a decision I did agree to think about it. That, in turn, resulted in a list of pros and cons which indicated more pros than cons.

Years later my daughter would chastise me for the unscientific method of evaluating an interpersonal relationship. "Apparently the pros didn't outweigh the cons by much," she said.

Bob was ecstatic after I told him soon thereafter that I would indeed agree to marry him. When we broke the news to his mother Bea she would not stop kissing me while holding me close.

"This is wonderful news," she gushed, tears cascading down her cheeks. "It's absolutely wonderful," she added, voice rising to an ear shattering pitch with the declaration: "I am so thrilled!"

She joked about how she would no longer have to feed Bob or iron his shirts. I responded with a little joke of my own. "I don't iron shirts."

She laughed and quickly changed the subject. "I insist you visit my cousin Sol in the Diamond Exchange on Forty-Seventh Street. I know he'll do right by you, even if you don't iron shirts."

Bea's mood abruptly changed. The cheerful bantering ceased.

"Bob," she said, "It is only right that we tell Lee about your little difficulty when you were younger—you know—when you were hospitalized." Bob's expression froze, clearly not expecting this revelation.

Ms. Freud pondered: Why was he hospitalized? Is there something wrong with him now? What other secrets are yet to be revealed?

Bea continued as if Bob were not in the room. "When Bob was 16 he became depressed and had to drop out of school..." her voice trailed off. Was she waiting for my reaction? Or for Bob to fill in the details?

But she continued quickly. "Bob received Electroconvulsive Therapy. The shock treatments worked remarkably well and he only missed six months of school." She made it sound as if Bob had been miraculously cured and suggested Bob introduce me to his psychiatrist. She was certain he would be thrilled to hear Bob was getting married.

I had no idea what to anticipate when we met with Dr. Oliver— and I was surprised by Bob's willingness to discuss the details of his hospitalization openly. Dr. Oliver asked if I had any concerns.

I confessed that what I knew about shock treatments was learned from the media, and that I found the process disturbing.

Dr. Oliver informed me that approximately 70 percent of those suffering from major depression—and do not respond to other treatments—get better with Electroconvulsive Therapy (ECT). He assured me that what Bob otherwise needed was someone to talk to.

After I left the office I felt somewhat relieved. I didn't realize then that our wedding music should be "Here Comes the Sucker," instead of "Here Comes the Bride."

CHAPTER THREE

An accepted marriage proposal, and now it was ring time.

Bob pre-selected three sparkling, pear-shaped diamonds from which to choose. I felt like Goldilocks deciding—big, bigger or biggest.

I lifted each bauble from the velvet pad and held it up to the florescent light. I did not want to appear piggish, but neither did I want to risk being mugged when I wore the ring.

I chose the mid-size stone, weighing approximately two carats. His cousin suggested Bob and I go to lunch while he mounted the stone in a platinum setting with tapered baguettes on either side. After Bob placed the ring on my finger I felt as if I would burst with joy. There was no doubt I had made the right decision.

At least you hope so, said Ms. Freud.

Until that moment the only thing that concerned me was Bob's periodic mood swings. I had never known anyone with a mercurial personality. I attributed his occasional arguments with his mother to immaturity. The excuse I made for his obsession with acquiring money was his desire to be a good provider. I had only to glance at my exquisite ring and all my concerns evaporated.

That was until we attended my friend's daughter's wedding and I discovered one more item for Bob's ever-increasing list of questionable behavior—impulsivity.

At one point during the reception Bob excused himself and interrupted the band leader. I assumed he was requesting our favorite song. Shortly after he returned, the band leader announced our engagement and upcoming wedding.

"Why did you do that?" I asked, visibly annoyed. "No one knows us here except the bride and her mother. Besides, this is their day, not ours."

I paused, and then asked rhetorically. "And when did we discuss a wedding date?"

"I did it because I felt like it," Bob replied—followed by sulking the rest of the evening.

My friends seemed perplexed at my decision to jump into another marriage soon after the divorce from Michelle's father. Although everyone understood how Bob contributed to my happiness I was reminded how I had often stated: "I'm not getting married again for a long, long time."

I knew Bob seemed too good to be true, but I was reluctant to reveal the real reason behind my decision to marry him. I told everyone he "swept me off my feet."

Truth was—I was a willing participant, enjoying every minute of my exciting new life.

Bea invited me to functions sponsored by organizations where she was a member and never missed an opportunity to introduce me as Bobby's fiancé. I joined her on shopping sprees where she insisted on buying me expensive outfits and appeared delighted when I wore them in the company of her friends. The attention made me feel special.

My mother and step-father were anxious to meet Bob. They invited us to fly to Florida to celebrate our engagement at a family gathering. Bob had little difficulty winning everybody over with his gift of gab and affable demeanor. My mother was particularly impressed by Bob's lustrous brown hair and his uncanny resemblance to my step-father.

Aside from Bob's refusal to wear his tie—insisting it remain hanging out of his breast pocket and Michelle's rolling her eyes in disapproval at everything Bob said or did—the trip was without incident.

Until we arrived home.

The taxi-stand was empty after our return flight arrived later than expected. Our only option was to rent a car. Bob complained all the way home while Michelle and I retreated to Dramamine induced semi-consciousness.

We were jolted awake when the car stopped abruptly, followed by the driver's door slamming. Bob was unable to find a parking space and had double-parked next to a fire hydrant. "Stay put!" he barked, as he grabbed the luggage and headed up the walkway toward our apartment building. Michelle and I obeyed and awaited his return.

But then we dozed, unaware that a police cruiser had parked behind us. By the time we realized the officer was writing a parking summons, Bob was already running toward the car, frantically waving and screaming a stream of expletives.

We were now fully alert, eyes widening as we strained to hear the heated exchange between Bob and the officer. We cowered, not knowing how the incident would play out. If Bob were arrested it would be my fault. I was consumed with guilt for dozing off.

Bob seethed as he reentered the car and threw the parking ticket in my face. Any attempt at an apology would have been akin to pouring a thimble of water on a raging fire. I prayed this was an isolated incident brought on by extreme circumstances—and would never occur again.

Naïve is as naïve does, observed Ms. Freud.

That night and for many nights to come.

CHAPTER FOUR

Bea began wedding plans from the time the ring was on my finger; she seized that prerogative by making it clear she would pay for everything.

I wanted a small intimate wedding. Bea envisioned a grandiose affair with hundreds of guests. My family and friends would barely occupy two tables at the reception. Her rationale was, "Why shouldn't you and Bob benefit from all the generous gifts I have given over the years? This is pay-back time."

At first my desire to keep the dog and pony show as low key as possible was overruled. I would feel uncomfortable with a traditional ceremony where the bride walks down the aisle. I imagined the whispers of the curious guests ogling the 35-year-old divorcee who was taking Bea's bachelor son off her hands. As well—and because I was not raised with strong religious beliefs—having a Rabbi conduct the ceremony was of little importance to me.

However, and since Bea felt that a Rabbi should officiate, I insisted on a reformed, English speaking Rabbi. She agreed to my request, but would not back down from her desire for a huge affair. After much negotiating we agreed Bob and I would be married in the Rabbi's study followed by the immediate family posing for formal pictures at the photographer's studio. When we arrived at the catering hall we would already be married.

But even as we proceeded toward the theoretically happy day, every so often a sense of dread enveloped me. I felt as if I were being propelled by some invisible force. Whenever Bob asked, "Are you happy," I hesitated before I answered but my inevitable reply was:

"Of course I'm happy. Who wouldn't be happy?"

Bob's response was as well always the same. "What are you afraid of? Do you think the sky will fall on you?"

After Bob assured me that would never happen, I felt foolish, but my instinctive sense of foreboding remained.

Hindsight reveals it should have been no surprise that Bob became increasingly lethargic in the two weeks before the wedding. Instead of feeling energized and excited, the lethargy was followed by a low-grade fever and even a loss in weight.

He in fact became bed-ridden.

Bob was tested for mononucleosis and a host of other maladies, but nothing was revealed. And although all test results were negative, he became dehydrated and spent one night in the hospital. In turn, he was advised to forget about leaving the country. We had been looking forward to a romantic honeymoon at "Las Brisas Resort," in Mexico. His doctor insisted Bob return for additional tests after the wedding.

During the time he was bed-ridden he broke a tooth which required an emergency dental visit. And further alarmed by the increasing deterioration, Bea contacted a physician's service that offered home visits.

After the doctor examined Bob, he announced flippantly, "I've seen this before. Your son has a case of 'cold feet' and if you want my advice you'll cancel the wedding."

This was not what we wanted to hear. Bea gave the doctor a tongue-lashing and sent him away. Bob assured us he was looking forward to our wedding day and fully expected to go through with it—even if he had to be carried to the Rabbi's study.

I began to have second thoughts, but didn't have the courage to back out.

Is it possible, asked Ms. Freud? Are you the one with cold feet?

I was grateful Bob was not on the brink of death, but by the time the big day arrived he had lost so much weight he needed suspenders to hold up his pants. And despite a weakened condition he forced a smile for the photographer and even attempted a few reception dance steps.

With the romantic honeymoon cancelled we arranged to stay at a motel. In the middle of the night Bob began perspiring profusely. We stripped the sheets and slept on the bedspread. I wanted to send for an ambulance or at least call Bea and ask what to do, but Bob would not allow me to call anyone. I spent most of the night applying cold compresses to his forehead.

When we awoke, the bedspread and the mattress were saturated with perspiration. It was as if a dam had burst releasing the toxins from Bob's body. He emerged a slightly weaker version of his old self, hungry for breakfast and already formulating plans to spend a few days at a resort upstate.

Maybe that doctor's cold feet theory was right, said Ms. Freud.

The married life that followed found us with an active social life, including organizing a "remarried" club. Many of our friends wished to continue the camaraderie enjoyed as members of the organization where we met our spouses.

Michelle continued to spend every other weekend with her father—which allowed Bob and me the opportunity to behave like carefree newlyweds. From all outward appearances we were a happy couple, raising a lovely young daughter. In reality being married to

Bob, working full-time, taking care of a home and raising a teenage daughter resembled a second-rate juggling act.

It was impossible to keep all the balls in the air at the same time. Not surprisingly, Bob was content with our arrangement:

1. A ready-made family.
2. A housekeeper.
3. A willing partner in bed.
4. And a woman who paid all her own and her daughter's expenses and never inquired about his finances.

Despite the outpouring of love and acceptance from Bob's family Michelle's allegiance remained with her father. I was certain she only tolerated Bob for my sake. Her disdain for him increased as his behavior became more bizarre. Michelle was resentful of Bob's presence and began acting out. She continued to spend every other weekend at her father's house which allowed Bob and me the opportunity to make plans and do as we pleased.

One of those plans involved a Washington's Birthday weekend in the Catskill Mountains. We invited Bea to join us, and looked forward to participating in winter sports and dressing up in the evening.

After we checked in the bellhop maneuvered a luggage cart through drafty connecting corridors while Bea chattered to no one in particular. When I dared to glance at Bob, I recognized his gloom and doom expression. A dark cloud was hovering; lightening wasn't far behind.

"Where in hell are we going?" Bob bellowed.

"We're almost there," the harried bellhop breathlessly replied.

"We better be!" Bob threatened.

After the cart came to a halt, the bellhop unlocked the door and began to unload luggage. Once inside we could clearly see this was not the "Ritz." The interior smelled musty and the chenille bedspread and parchment window shades were what one would expect to find at the "Bates Motel." The rest of the furnishings were remnants of a bygone era.

"You have to be kidding. This is it?" Bob asked, incredulously.

Before the bellhop could answer, Bob dialed the front desk. After a heated discussion, he slammed the phone and announced, "We're leaving!"

The bellhop reloaded luggage onto the cart and in silence we retraced the lengthy journey. When we reached the lobby the bellhop innocently inquired, "What should I do with the luggage?" Before Bob could say something inappropriate Bea thanked the bellhop for his trouble and gave him several dollars.

Bob was now perspiring profusely, his face the color of freshly cooked beets. Bea ordered him to sit down and calm himself. After Bob threw himself into an overstuffed chair, she headed toward the reservation desk.

And you chose to stand between the pouting child and the woman who could charm the pants off an already undressed snake, observed Ms. Freud.

Within seconds Bea turned toward us waving a room key. This time we had only to walk a short distance to the elevator before reaching a room befitting what I was reluctantly beginning to acknowledge was the mood-monster—and his entourage.

CHAPTER FIVE

When Bob and I first met he weighed 250 pounds and his total cholesterol was 330. He confided that his secret desire was to be thin enough to wear a jumpsuit, fashionable at that time.

Bob had little knowledge of nutrition or portion control and since I had battled the bulge most of my life I was able to guide him through the weight-loss process.

His biggest obstacle was the family ritual of eating a snack before bedtime. He did not understand the connection between eating bread with butter and cheese every night and his father's untimely death at the age of 56. It was after a late night snack his dad was found sitting on the toilet, a newspaper dangling from lifeless fingers.

Bob's late night eating habit began to interfere with our relationship. He expected a fourth meal while my energy was depleted and I was ready to crawl into bed. If I refused to prepare Bob's snack he pouted. If I gave in to his request I pouted. No matter how you looked at it, it was a lose-lose situation—except around the waistline.

After attending a fund-raiser at the Pierre Hotel, I could not wait to kick off my heels, unzip my gown and climb into bed. During the ride home, Bob mumbled something about feeling hungry.

"You must be out of your mind!" I exclaimed. "You are sadly mistaken if you think I'm stepping foot in the kitchen when I get home."

When Bob suggested we stop at a 24-hour diner I was too tired to argue. The waitress took our order—tea and an English muffin for me and a grilled cheese sandwich with French fries and a large Coke for my companion in the tuxedo.

And he savored every morsel, said Ms. Freud, licking his fingers instead of using a napkin.

When we arrived home at 3 a.m. Bob was perplexed when I rebuffed his amorous gestures. The only thing I had on my mind as I pushed past him and flopped into bed was it was either me or the sandwich and he had already had the sandwich.

And I could never understand why Bea sabotaged his attempts to lose weight and even hid chocolate bars behind the fruit in her refrigerator. She barely ate a morsel and was thin as Popeye's girlfriend "Olive Oil." Her cooking was hard to resist and additional servings were readily available. She believed corn and mashed potatoes sufficed as vegetables and considered Jell-O topped with a mountain of Cool Whip a low-calorie dessert.

We were having dinner at Bea's house when Bob proudly announced, "I don't need bread to sop up gravy because I no longer eat gravy." He demonstrated how he had learned to use his knife to push food onto his fork.

Instead of praising the effort, Bea addressed him, sarcastically, "You'll see, eventually you'll gain back the weight you lost." I was stunned and hurt by her insensitivity. It was obvious from the pained expression on Bob's face he agreed.

And another thing she did was even more peculiar, said Ms. Freud.

When Bob became riled up and an unpleasant scene was imminent, she would purse her lips, bat heavily made-up eyelashes and say:

"Bobby—be a good boy and I'll buy you something."

He reacted to those words as if hearing a post-hypnotic suggestion. Hands at his sides and eyes cast downward, he snapped to attention.

What warped game were they playing Ms. Freud wondered?

I finally found the courage to ask Bob what was going on.

Bob leapt immediately to whining. "Ever since I can remember she made that promise whenever she wanted me to behave. I hated when she did that. She never kept her promise, but I always fell for it—even now."

After I pointed out he was no longer a child I never mentioned the subject again, but whenever I witnessed this interaction I found it disturbing.

Bea began dating a lovely man she had socialized with while respective spouses were alive. Ernie was easy-going and soft-spoken—an interesting addition to this lively family. Bob and I were not surprised when marriage plans were announced. We welcomed Ernie and his grown children into the family. Bob seemed genuinely happy his mother had found a new life partner.

In other family matters, when Bob and his brother were together they appeared to share a close relationship. However, Bob once acknowledged a great deal of animosity toward Allan. Bob was expected to work in the family business on Saturdays and during school vacations—while Bob said Allan hung around reading comic books.

I told Bob to get over it. I experienced a similar situation with my brother when I had to baby-sit him all the time.

But Bob's resentment was soon revealed as more than sibling rivalry. He revealed a family secret which I would later discover was one of many. I listened intently as a lifetime of resentment unfolded.

Allan fancied himself an entrepreneur and dabbled in a series of unsuccessful business ventures. Bea kept him afloat by acting as his financial guardian angel. She believed if she did not help him he would fall into a deep depression that would ultimately destroy his marriage. Bob felt his brother received all the breaks while he had to bust his back to earn a living.

"It isn't fair," Bob often lamented.

"Have you tried to explain how you feel to your mother?"

"Bull shit! That doesn't help. Whenever I've tried to talk to her she tells me not to worry."

Bob was also afraid he would have to wait until Bea died before receiving any money from his father's life insurance policy. Bea and both sons had been named beneficiaries. The family lawyer convinced her that the boys were too young to manage money. He in turn advised the sons to sign over the insurance proceeds to her.

He resented Bea as well for other perceived injustices. He recalled her putting him to bed while it was still light outside. Her excuse was that his father worked hard all day and after he arrived home deserved peace and quiet. Bob believed Bea didn't allow him to stay up later because she wanted his father all to herself.

The relationship with his mother always raised some questions about the boy who was now a man—and with hindsight provided a few answers about the man who was often a boy.

CHAPTER SIX

As Bob's behavior became more dysfunctional, it really wasn't a surprise to find that he wanted to keep tabs on me after my gynecologist recommended I have a tubal ligation rather than continue to take birth control pills.

We had already agreed not to create a child—and he found the added bonus of my becoming a "sex machine" very appealing. However, that also led to his insistence that I account for every minute of the day and to include him in all my plans.

I had recently returned to college two nights a week to complete my bachelor's degree. Bob insisted on tagging along. He planned to relax in the college library and then meet me at the end of class.

However, after my second class was cancelled one evening, I headed toward the library expecting to find Bob reading or dozing in a quiet corner.

He was nowhere to be found.

I hurried down the stairs thinking he may already be on his way to the social sciences building. I thought it best to wait under the rotunda where the main entrance was visible from my vantage point.

I was surprised to see Bob's car entering the campus from outside.

And he's coming from where, asked Ms. Freud?

I considered the possibilities and did my best to push the most disturbing ones out of my thoughts. I raced down the stairs and entered the car.

"What are you doing over here?" he asked puzzled.

"What are you doing coming from the outside?" I inquired suspiciously. I assumed he would lie about his whereabouts. After carefully weighing his words Bob offered a simple explanation.

"I often leave campus, but I make sure to return in time to pick you up."

"Where in hell do you go?"

"To the movies—to see porno flicks—that's all."

"You go where?" I asked incredulously.

After the initial shock, I did not know whether to laugh or cry. On one hand Bob had been lying about waiting for me in the library, but on the other hand he was increasing his love making repertoire. My anger and suspicion slowly dissipated and I attributed these harmless escapades to the old adage, "boys will be boys."

Bob was highly sexualized so it came as no surprise that he also became acquainted with a young couple who frequented "Plato's Retreat." For all I knew he was already intimately involved with this couple before he proposed that I join them. Bob was excited at the prospect of me accompanying him and assured me we could remain spectators if we chose not to participate in sexual activities.

"It's nothing like you imagine. It's a happening, the same as Woodstock." Bob explained.

I mused: "I heard Woodstock was a pretty wild scene."

"You don't have to do anything you don't want to," he reassured me.

I was fully aware of all the negative publicity "Plato's" had received, but here was my beloved extolling the virtues of an adult social club where:

1. A visitor could remain wrapped in a towel.
2. Partake of a sumptuous buffet.
3. Or participate in a *ménage à trios.*

Bob sounded like the head counselor at a summer camp trying to convince the non-swimmers to jump into a cesspool. I did my best to avoid the subject and eventually discussions regarding "Plato's" ceased.

Nonetheless, Bob's demands to spend time together bordered on obsession. He didn't understand in addition to cleaning, shopping and laundry I had to complete homework assignments. Saturday mornings were usually devoted to household chores. Bob constantly interrupted, inquiring how much longer before I would be ready to leave. As the pressure to increase our "togetherness" intensified I cleaned less.

Bob came up with what he thought was the perfect solution for spending more time with him. On days when schools were closed I would accompany him to sales appointments. He suggested I bring my textbooks and work on my assignments while he drove. After he reached his destination Bob would insist I stay in the locked car.

And no matter what the weather, noted Ms. Freud, you waited like a faithful pet longing for your master's return.

One bitterly cold day I could not wait any longer; I needed to use the restroom. I ventured inside the building adjacent to the parking lot. After I exited the restroom, I saw Bob engaged in what appeared to be an intimate conversation with the post-pubescent receptionist. They were leaning into each other, his hand on her shoulder as she seductively tossed long, blonde hair.

When Bob realized I was watching he became enraged and admonished me for not waiting in the car. When I tried to explain why I was in the building he dismissed me with an angry hand wave while stomping past me toward the front door.

If he had a rolled up newspaper he would have hit you on the nose, noted Ms. Freud—and still you remained.

Planning weekend activities in general became a major issue. Usually, Bob wanted to know by Thursday what I had planned. Despite my busy schedule I made every effort to provide a detailed itinerary covering meal times, if we would eat in or out, whether we were socializing with friends, movie reviews and show times, a weather report and scheduled rest periods.

I did everything possible to keep Bob from becoming over-wrought or anxious, but his bizarre behavior escalated along with his need to know the schedule for the upcoming weekend well before Thursday. During dinner I noticed him glaring at me. I stared into my plate and continued to eat.

"Have you decided what we're doing this weekend," he inquired.

"It's only Tuesday. We just finished the weekend. It takes time to…"

Before I completed the thought, he banged the table. "I don't understand? What difference does it make what day it is," he yelled? "You make such a big deal out of everything."

"You'll have to be patient. I need more time."

Now it was his turn to stare at his plate and pick at food.

Good, he's pouting, Ms. Freud smiled. At least now he'll leave you alone.

CHAPTER SEVEN

Michelle and I had moved into a new apartment shortly before I met Bob. After we were married, we agreed not to disrupt her education by moving to a new school district—but his incessant comments about the glory of home ownership were a constant complaint about "how stupid" we were for paying rent.

I saw it differently. I had been an apartment dweller my entire life and had no desire to be burdened with the expense or time required to look after a house.

Besides, it wouldn't be much longer before Michelle would be out of the house, Ms. Freud reasoned.

On the other hand Bob had always lived in a house and believed home ownership was not only economically prudent, but mandatory. But he was unrealistic in the desire to move to the affluent neighborhood adjacent to where we lived. Even if we could manage the mortgage we would be "house poor." It would be impossible to keep up with the Joneses and would prove to be a miserable existence, a decision I was certain we would regret.

Occasionally, I appeased Bob by accompanying a realtor who understood our dilemma. He drove us to a sad little rundown house where the owners were highly motivated. They were embroiled in a divorce, anxious for a quick sale.

The broker suggested we make a low-ball offer. If the owners accepted, we could remodel with money saved on the purchase price. We followed his advice and after much sweat and hard work managed to turn the sow's ear into a polyester purse.

But happily ever after did not follow, said Ms. Freud.

At the time I did not understand how difficult it would be for Bob to keep up with the bills and deal with responsibilities of home ownership. I had experience living on my own and knew how to make a dollar out of 99 cents. However, and because he always had Bea to fall back on, Bob's money management skills were deficient, and caused him anxiety. We in turn devised a plan to ease that anxiety.

The plan was that Bob would pay for all basic expenses and save money toward our retirement; I in turn would pay for my personal expenses and Michelle's expenses—as well as, entertainment and vacations.

What you actually did was devise a business arrangement, Ms. Freud said, and with Bob as the senior partner who controlled most of the money.

The inspection report on the newly acquired and 50-year-old frame house recommended that we replace the hot water heater and caulk the windows. There was no evidence of termite activity or structural defect.

The interior needed to be updated.

Especially the lavender bathroom fixtures and black and white floor tiles, said Ms. Freud. Whenever you entered the room you imagined a voice yelling: I'm old and ugly—do something!

In order to detract from the unpleasantness I covered the floor with a shag rug cut to fit around the commode and sink. Next, I matted and framed three prints depicting a feline family using the "facilities." I had hoped after Bob noticed the improvement he would compliment me on my decorating skills. Instead he came storming out of the bathroom stark naked, shaking the new lavender towels in the air, cursing furiously. He complained the towels were not absorbing moisture fast enough.

"Where in hell did you find these crappy towels? What did you do, buy the cheapest towels you could find?" Bob pushed past me into the bedroom, grabbed money off the dresser and tossed it at me.

"If you needed more money you should have asked for it. Now buy real towels, not this crap!" With that, Bob threw the towel on top of the money at my feet.

His anger surged suddenly and disappeared just as quickly. After he quieted down and I stopped crying I retrieved the money. Although I planned to purchase new towels for Bob, I continued using the towels that were the target of his rant.

Nothing wrong with those damn towels, said Ms. Freud.

Other altercations often involved what he thought Michelle should be allowed to do or not do. He was adamant about her not having friends sleep over because he was not allowed to when he was a teenager. At times Bob seemed preoccupied with Michelle's sex life and often asked inappropriate questions. "Do you think she is having sex? Is she on the pill?"

Which is why it was more than surreal one day in the laundry room, mused Ms. Freud.

I never asked Bob for help with the family laundry, and I was on the phone when the buzzer announced the dryer had stopped. I hung up and proceeded to the basement.

The scene that greeted me found Bob in front of the clothes dryer selecting specific articles of clothing. I was shocked when I witnessed him caressing Michelle's silk bikini panties.

I exploded in his ear. "If you're thinking of touching my daughter you don't have to worry about me hurting you. She will kill you herself!"

I expected him to be remorseful, offer an apology, anything. Instead he walked past me and continued up the stairs without saying a word.

I was aware that incest was a common occurrence. The media had done a thorough job of educating the public, particularly when a step-father and step-daughter are involved. I was satisfied knowing I had made my suspicions clear and I planned to remain hyper-vigilant in the future.

What else could you do, Ms. Freud challenged? And what if you were mistaken about what you witnessed?

At the same time, I also had no doubt that Bob was self-righteously paranoid. He created scenes in restaurants when he accused the hostess of singling him out by seating him at the worst table or giving him a different menu than everyone else. He would also insist on doing favors for people and afterwards complain those same persons were taking advantage of him.

Bob's lack of judgment in general was a problem. He had a habit of not monitoring the toaster-oven. On more than one occasion when I entered the kitchen, flames were licking at the charred remains of a roll. I feared the wooden cabinets would catch on fire.

"Bob, do something!" I shrieked. "Take the toaster-oven outside and let the fire burn out."

Bob looked up from his newspaper and calmly responded, "I'm wearing my slippers. I have to go upstairs and put on shoes."

I threw open the back door, pulled out the plug and grabbed the flaming appliance with a dish rag. My lungs filled with acrid fumes as I ran onto the porch, raised the toaster-oven high above my head and tossed it onto the concrete. Debris scattered everywhere.

Bob stood in the doorway watching me. "You didn't have to do that; you could have waited for me."

At another time, we were on vacation when the fire alarm went off in the middle of the night. A computerized voice instructed us to evacuate. Instead of throwing on a bathrobe, Bob insisted on getting dressed. I fled down the fire stairs and left him in the room.

When the firemen searched, Bob was found rummaging in the closet unsure of what to wear. Fortunately the incident turned out to be a false alarm—unlike the internal alarms I had been ignoring almost from the moment I met Bob.

CHAPTER EIGHT

Bob's view of the world was distorted and he was easily impressed.

"My friend drives a Mercedes 600S," he would announce proudly.

And he would make such an announcement even if he had never met the owner, but only observed a man entering the car in a parking lot. He was also self-righteously convinced that if somebody's house was bigger than ours, or if someone drove an expensive car, the owner had to be involved in illegal activity.

The tension in our ever more dysfunctional home was palpable and Michelle spent less time at home—if for no other reason than the bizarre greeting scene Bob insisted upon each time she came home.

If Bob and I were seated on the couch, and when we heard her key in the lock, he would bolt across the room even before the door opened.

The same awkward scene played out over and over. No matter how hard Michelle tried to deflect Bob's embrace, he never failed to grab her in a bear hug before she could extricate herself and flee up the stairs to her bedroom. I remained seated, as if frozen in place. I knew if I jumped up to greet her it would have only added to her discomfort.

What kind of mother are you to allow these encounters to continue, Ms. Freud questioned? Perhaps she's unaware how helpless you are.

It pained me to know how uncomfortable she must have felt and I wondered why she never looked toward me for help—but one day I made up my mind that the next time Michelle entered the house I would be the one to hug and kiss her even if I had to wrestle Bob to the floor.

I was poised to spring the next time I heard her on the front porch—but Bob was already up and across the room. With both of us approaching, Michelle's gaze found my face and I detected the look of a trapped animal

She bolted up the stairs, slamming the door behind her.

I sprinted up the stairs, two at a time, and rapped on her door.

No response.

I opened the door hesitantly and found her sitting cross-legged on the bed. I felt as if we were two strangers meeting for the first time—but after I held out my arms she rose and we embraced. In that one delicious moment I knew our mother-daughter bond would never be broken. Nothing would ever come between us, not even Bob.

The moment of bliss was interrupted by a knock, followed by Bob asking, "May I come in?"

Michelle and I stared at one another, stunned and unable to respond. He entered the room and leaned against the dresser satisfied to stand there—grinning like the village idiot. The awkward silence ended when I abruptly left the room, Bob trailing closely behind.

Bob's possessiveness of my space and time only increased when later, I received a phone call informing me Michelle had been rushed to the emergency room at Lenox Hill Hospital. She had excruciating abdominal pain and was running a fever. The official diagnosis was a combination of food poisoning and a previously undiagnosed ovarian cyst—which could be treated with a course of antibiotics.

I wanted to spend the following day with Michelle, but Bob talked me out of it. He argued that nothing would be accomplished by sitting in a hospital room all day. He did not understand—my baby was all alone and I wanted to be with her. Bob insisted we visit her together, joined at the hip, for the balance of her hospital stay.

PART TWO

ON THE
MERRY-GO-ROUND

CHAPTER NINE

Every other year Bob and I looked forward to an expensive vacation.

Paid for by yours truly, said Ms. Freud.

My ego enjoyed hearing Bob brag about my skills as his personal travel agent. Occupied with planning a trip, I in fact did not dwell on my miserable marriage. And by researching the itinerary in advance I believed I could reduce the possibility that Bob would flip out during the vacation.

And you thought you could keep the mood monster at bay, smirked Ms. Freud.

After stopping in Atlanta, Georgia to watch my brother run the annual Peachtree 10k Run, we continued on to that year's destination—New Orleans. My friend Laura had recommended a quaint hotel in the French Quarter, once a brothel frequented by lusty pirates. Locals believed those men haunted the hotel. I wasn't sure if it was the word brothel—or the thought of virile pirates that aroused Bob—but that night he made love as if possessed.

We visited all the popular tourist attractions, stuffed ourselves with beignets, dined at Court of the Two Sisters and pigged-out on Bananas Foster at Brennan's. After a relaxing riverboat cruise we rode the St. Charles streetcar to the zoo.

***And leave it to Bob to photograph two zebras fornicating,
Ms. Freud sighed.***

When the male zebra sensed us, he charged; Bob and I almost knocked one another to the ground attempting to escape.

After a long day of sightseeing we found it impossible to cool off in the hotel pool; the tepid water offered little relief. We had no choice but retreat to the air-conditioned hotel room for an afternoon delight, followed by a nap.

But as the week wore on, Bob became increasingly disoriented. Whenever we exited a building he walked in the wrong direction. When I attempted to redirect him by pointing to the map in the tourist guide he became abusive and accused me of not knowing what I was talking about. During one such incident I pointed toward the riverboat, clearly visible from where we were standing.

"See…there's…the…river…," I said slowly, as if speaking to a child. "And…here…we…are…on…the…map."

He responded by heading in the opposite direction. I stood alone in the sweltering heat, tempted to let him continue on until he realized he was lost. But after he slowed down I ran toward him, took his arm and guided him toward the hotel.

Whenever we were on vacation Bob obsessed over buying souvenirs for friends and relatives. He spent a great deal of time comparison shopping and agonized over which souvenir to choose for each person. But true to self-righteous form, after he made his decision and we were on our way out of the store, he was certain the shopkeeper had ripped him off.

On this trip, many of the souvenirs were fragile. I suggested we divide items between both suitcases. I placed one open suitcase on either side of the bed to avoid getting in each other's way. Bob quickly gathered the souvenirs and placed them in a pile at his feet.

When I restated the logical packing plan, I could have just as well been speaking in tongues.

"I want the souvenirs all together in one bag," Bob demanded.

"You've got to be kidding!"

"That's the way I want it."

"You can't possibly be that stupid. Can't you see how ridiculous it is to do it your way?"

I watched in disbelief as Bob loaded the souvenirs haphazardly, completely disregarding what I had said. He slammed the over-stuffed suitcase shut. I walked around to where he was standing and tried to lift the suitcase, but it would not budge.

"What happens when the suitcase breaks open and all your precious souvenirs fall out?"

"I don't care," Bob fired back. "Leave it the way it is!"

We were running out of time. I found it difficult to reduce myself to his yelling and carping level, but somebody had to take charge.

"Get the hell away from that suitcase!" I commanded. Bob reacted as if jolted by electricity. He jumped onto the bed and sat on his haunches.

"Don't you dare move until I say so," I warned.

I packed the two suitcases, interspersing souvenirs between articles of clothing. Bob neither moved nor spoke until I instructed him to get dressed and only then did he dare ask, "What should I wear?"

I was convinced the stress of the trip in itself did not cause Bob's meltdown. And that belief was confirmed as we approached our house where we were greeted by strange noises coming from the backyard.

I imagined little elves from a childhood fairy tale "tap-tap-tapping" with tiny hammers. In fact, there was a construction crew working feverishly in an attempt to complete a task scheduled without my knowledge—and apparently the work was behind schedule because when the workmen saw a look of exasperation on Bob's face and the shocked expression on mine one of them exclaimed: "Oh shit, they're home already!"

The pressure of keeping the project secret and Bob worrying how I would react must have been overwhelming. Many discussions, debates and arguments about building a deck had preceded this day. I did not want it and we did not need it. That was compounded by it taking up the entire backyard, and us rarely being home to use it.

Bob had offered only one argument. "I want it!"

Now we had it.

Not knowing how Bob was handling our finances irked me endlessly—and to make matters worse he also insisted I give him receipts from our restaurant dinners to submit with his expense reports. Not wishing to make him angry, I hated it, but assented —our *Big Lie*, literally feeding his little lie.

What you hated more, Ms. Freud said, was feeling helpless.

And with life moving forward and getting more complicated, that reality would only get worse.

CHAPTER TEN

Michelle began dating a young man she met in college. Bob and I were impressed with Eric's outgoing personality, intelligence and good looks. She had only alluded that his parents were financially comfortable.

After meeting Eric's parents Bob became fixated on how the wealth had been acquired. However, there was no mystery; savvy business people had worked long and hard—and earned the lifestyle.

But with each successive meeting Bob's agitation increased. He concluded in fact that ownership of a boat by Eric's parent meant involvement in illegal drug transportation.

I tried to ignore this mindless accusation, along with his obvious attempt to emulate the social circle. He purchased Cole Haan loafers and a pair of boat shoes—which he wore, sans socks, even during the winter.

But I could not have been more pleased when Michelle announced Eric had proposed during a romantic horse-drawn carriage ride through Central Park.

Early in our marriage Bob had assured me we had a Treasury Note set aside for Michelle's future. When it became clear the catered affair we were planning would require a considerable amount of money, Bob denied the money for Michelle ever existed. And then without even attempting to rationalize his accusations of illegal drug sales providing money to Eric's family, he insisted that Eric's family should pay for the entire wedding.

After the announcement, Michelle began her quest for the perfect wedding gown. Saturdays were devoted to visiting bridal shops. She also scoured bridal magazines to update her list before each outing. I was relieved when the exhausting search ended—until I read the price tag dangling from the gown she had selected.

"Three thousand dollars!" resounded in my head, but when she stepped out of the dressing room in the gown of her dreams she resembled a fairy tale princess.

"The gown is incredible. You look incredible," I gushed, trying not to mention the outrageous price tag—the cost of looking incredible.

I vowed to give her choice serious consideration, but I was already agonizing over what I would say to Bob. When I told him the gown Michelle chose would cost $3,000—the same amount he had spent on the deck—he did not hesitate for a moment before insisting he'd pay for it. Of course, there was no mention of who would pay for my gown. What was most important was that the wedding plans proceed smoothly.

Eventually we agreed that Eric's parents, Michelle's father, Bob and I would each pay a portion of the wedding expenses. In order to come up with our share Bob convinced me to co-sign a home equity loan. The available line of credit was considerably more than our wedding obligation. When I brought this to Bob's attention he became enraged and I withdrew into survival mode—being selectively mute.

And instead of renting one from the party store, Bob insisted on building the "wishing well" for Michelle's surprise bridal shower. The task proved more difficult than he imagined—which predictably resulted in hours of bitching and moaning.

Michelle was genuinely surprised later when she entered the restaurant where friends and family waited. She received lovely gifts which included revealing lingerie. Each time she unwrapped a gift, a chorus of "oohs" and "aahs" resounded. But when she held the lingerie under her chin the expression on Bob's face concerned me.

The following day I was surprised when he in turn presented me a shopping bag from "Victoria's Secret." Bob had never given me a gift unless it was an occasion. His eyes gleamed as he watched me remove tissue paper from the pink shopping bag—only to discover a duplicate of the most risqué lingerie Michelle received at her bridal shower.

I was not flattered. I refused to participate in Bob's sick fantasy and exchanged the gift for one I hoped would not remind him of his step-daughter.

Bob's obsessive over-involvement in the wedding plans became intrusive. He went as far as to argue how to slice and serve the chateau brian and followed that by an irrational harangue upon receiving a reminder note from the caterer about an additional deposit being required.

"Who does he think he is? Doesn't he have enough of my money?"

I tried to make Bob understand he did not have a choice, but he pledged to withhold further payment until the wedding day.

"He'll have to whistle before he gets another penny out of me!" he yelled.

I preferred to deal with the embarrassment of showing up alone rather than risk ruining Michelle's special day.

"I can't deal with this—with you," I said. "Don't send the caterer another cent. Don't come at all!"

"What will you do for money?"

"Between my father, my brother and a credit card advance we'll manage just fine without you."

Bob appeared panic-stricken as I reached for the telephone. He grabbed the receiver and begged me not to call my family. After an insincere apology he begrudgingly wrote a check to the caterer.

He also became increasingly anxious about paying the final bill. He was personally responsible for the wedding expenses after insisting upon signing the contracts. He went so far as to purchase a money belt to wear under his tuxedo and agonized over whether the other parents would come up with the agreed upon sums—and what if this, and what if that.

You thought you would scream, said Ms. Freud.

My dad and brother were flying in for the wedding. I made reservations at a nearby motel. It would have been impossible to have them under the same roof with Bob when he was on the verge of a major meltdown—but that didn't stop the inevitable.

My brother was helping our dad select a tie when Bob and I arrived to pick them up for dinner. The momentary delay was more than Bob could tolerate. He released an onslaught of insults and chastised my father for keeping him waiting. I was used to Bob's outbursts, but everyone else looked stunned. My dad quickly grabbed a tie and knotted it with trembling fingers.

"My father doesn't deserve to be treated this way," I said with barely controlled anger. "Because you are impatient he has to be demeaned and humiliated!" I demanded.

No response.

My dad and brother stood frozen, afraid that words would exacerbate the volatile situation.

"Apologize to my father!" I demanded.

"It's all right—it's all right," my father pleaded. "He doesn't have to apologize. Let's just go to dinner." As my dad turned to leave, I touched his shoulder.

"No Daddy. You don't understand. He has to apologize."

All eyes were on Bob. Watching. Waiting. Finally, with halting speech, and in a barely audible voice, Bob said, "I'm sorry."

On the day of the wedding tension mounted as I attended to details and seating snafus. The Rabbi arrived late. Michelle was stung by a bee and Eric chewed the inside of his mouth until it bled—but nothing prepared me for what Bob had in store for us.

He literally ordered everyone around.

"Go this way!" or "Do it that way!" and at one point, he shouted at nobody in particular, "Listen to me—just listen to me!" It was not a pretty sight—the mind's eye equivalent of a red-faced toddler, lying on the floor, arms flailing, kicking his feet.

The rest of the day was a blur. It ended with me sitting on the edge of the bathtub in Eric and Michelle's apartment, dressed in my mother-of-the-bride gown and sobbing uncontrollably.

After noticing my long absence, Eric knocked. He cautiously peered in and placed a comforting hand on my shoulder. He had no way of knowing how prophetic his words were when he assured me, "It's all over now."

The photographer had been a thorn in Bob's side from the moment we viewed the wedding proofs. Bob ranted about how underrepresented he was in relation to how much money he spent—and that despite the home equity loan I was coerced into co-signing making us equal participants.

The least he could have done was include you in his rants about how much the wedding cost, Ms. Freud muttered.

After Michelle and Eric presented a beautiful parent's album, Bob plotted his revenge. He threatened to get even with the photographer by harming his car or destroying his camera equipment. I knew Bob was capable of violence and I feared he would make good on the threats. He wanted to know where the photographer lived and what type of car he drove but backed down when I suggested he ask Michele and Eric for the information.

Years later I discovered Bob had told acquaintances he had paid for the entire wedding. I felt better after I set the record straight; I made sure everyone knew he contributed a portion of the money along with the other parents.

Bob continued to be preoccupied with money. It did not matter whose money it was. He was consumed with thoughts of making it, accumulating it, counting it and moving it from one bank to another to earn a fraction of a percent more interest.

He was convinced the only way to attain true wealth was to be in business for himself. He would often bring home information about a franchise or "pyramid" scheme that sounded too good to be true. I was the voice of reason. I analyzed the information and explained a scheme was not practical and would result in losing his investment.

The one time he made a business decision without consulting me was when he purchased experimental manufacturing equipment which he hid in the garage. Bob confided in Eric that he had changed the lock, afraid that if I found out what he had done I would kill him.

Locks and life—and the *Big Lie* continued.

CHAPTER ELEVEN

Life went on—including the shock of learning my mother had breast cancer. I flew down to be with her, and slept in a chair at her bedside the night before surgery. I hoped my presence would be comforting.

After I returned home her phone calls and letters sounded hopeful. My mind was focused on my own life and I didn't pay much attention when she complained about aching bones.

We were unaware the cancer had metastasized. Six months after surgery she fell into a coma and died. There were words that went unspoken and issues that would never be resolved. It was not a good time for me.

There is never a good time for death, said Ms. Freud, and certainly not for the deceased.

I told Michelle and Eric it was unnecessary to take time off from work. Bob and I would be flying home the day after the funeral. A friend of the family ordered platters of food for the Shiva. It was customary to gather at the home of a family member after the funeral where mourners consoled each other and paid tribute to the deceased.

Bob walked aimlessly from room to room as the long period of inactivity and civility wore on. I suggested he take a break and pick up a couple of items that were almost depleted. He appeared relieved at the prospect of escaping, but I did not answer quickly enough after he asked how much coleslaw he should buy. His face twisted into a grimace.

"God damn it, answer me already. I can't wait here forever until you make up your mind!"

The mourners stopped talking in mid-sentence and paused to listen to the drama that was unfolding. I felt mortified as I crooked a finger and beckoned Bob to follow me onto the catwalk outside the apartment.

"If you ever speak to me in front of anyone in that tone of voice, I will kick you in the shins and bring you to your knees. Do you understand?"

Bob nodded.

"Now, buy one large bag of ice and two pounds of coleslaw and after you return, mind your mouth."

Once again, he nodded.

I had hoped the incident would be forgotten by the time Bob returned until I saw pity in everyone's eyes. I imagined them wondering, what has poor Lee saddled herself with? Her mother must be turning over in her grave.

I couldn't get back to our hotel room fast enough. Within seconds of climbing into bed Bob pressed his body against mine while pushing up my nightgown. He ignored my attempts to pull away and continued to grope me with a sense of urgency. I was incapable of responding.

"I'm grieving for God's sake!"

"What does one thing have to do with the other? I only wanted to make you feel better."

"Don't you mean it would make you feel better?"

Thankfully, the groping ceased—but the nightmare was far from over.

CHAPTER TWELVE

It was not unusual for Bob to arrive home before I did. Occasionally I would discover envelopes addressed to me ripped open. When I questioned him the excuse was always the same.

"I didn't realize it was for you. I opened it by mistake."

I was getting used to not having privacy. I often heard "click" during telephone conversations, accompanied by the sound of Bob's breathing on the extension phone. Before going to bed each night I deliberately arranged the items in my handbag in a specific order. In the morning there was no doubt he had rifled through the contents.

"I was just looking for a nail file," was often the reason he gave for snooping.

Was it his guilt that prompted him to suspect you of hiding something, Ms. Freud mused? Or was it his paranoia—and did it really matter?

Bob was illogical and unpredictable. This included violent outbursts, periods of melancholia and depression. Stress exacerbated these situations. When he was good he was very, very good, but when he was bad....

I became increasingly alarmed by his behavior. Once when somebody parked too close to his car I had to restrain him from breaking the offender's windshield with a tire iron. On another occasion he borrowed my lipstick and scribbled obscenities on the windshield of the offending car. Bob would fly into an explosive rage if he found a scratch on my car or if I did not hold a flashlight in just the right position when he experienced difficulty completing a simple task—like screwing in a light bulb.

And he threatened me on a regular basis, "Watch out for the white powder in your coffee" implying he had poisoned it—or "I'm going to break your eyeglasses," when I was reading.

Or sometimes he would storm into the kitchen without warning. "I want to talk to you unless you choke to death first," he'd say and then abruptly leave without another word.

I was surprised when Bob invited Michelle and Eric to celebrate my birthday at a waterfront restaurant. Eric offered to drive after he sensed Bob's agitation. Michelle suggested I sit in the front away from Bob. He demanded I move my seat forward. After I released the lever he kicked the back of my seat. I stifled the impulse to cry out when I struck my shoulder on the dashboard.

Michelle became visibly upset. She started to ask if I was hurt, but I raised my hand to silence her. I was still in denial about how unbearable my life had become.

After we entered the restaurant Eric and Michelle checked on our brunch reservation. Bob reached out and pushed me into the wall of an unattended coatroom. I was momentarily startled, but I struggled to maintain my balance. I no longer reacted when Bob lashed out. I had become anesthetized.

Developing co-dependency survival skills, said Ms. Freud.

Winter presented other problems. Bob's depression became pervasive and he found it difficult to function. Getting out of bed to prepare for work took tremendous effort. His winter malaise dramatically impacted our relationship. I would often find him in bed in the fetal position, silently weeping. His inert form tightly wrapped in his robe resembled a larvae encased in its cocoon. Each winter the cycle began anew.

While researching journal articles for my Psychopathology course I uncovered a definite correlation between what I read and the behavior Bob exhibited. Seasonal Affective Disorder (SAD) which affects more than a half-million Americans is related to the change in seasons. The length of daylight affects the level of serotonin in the brain which in turn alters the circadian rhythm. Increased exposure to daylight or "bright-light" therapy offers some relief. However, someone who is vulnerable to bipolar disorder may experience severe manic symptoms when exposed to too much light.

Despite my method for alleviating depression—become proactive, develop a plan and execute the plan—Bob's winter doldrums were beginning to rub off on me. I could not keep shutting down physically and emotionally each winter and come back to life in the spring when Bob rejoined the human race. His cycling was destroying me. Our marriage would not survive without professional help.

We were engaged in another predictable Sunday morning discussion. "It's not your fault!" Bob insisted for the umpteen-millionth time, "I know it's my fault," as if assuming responsibility would sustain me through another lonely, lifeless winter.

"I won't survive another winter with you; if I go through this once more I will surely die," I sobbed until the last bit of emotion drained from me.

We stared at each other for what seemed like an eternity, two empty vessels devoid of life's energy, withered, worthless. When I remembered my remedy for depression, I left the room in search of the telephone directory.

Bob's anxious voice followed me. "What are you doing?"

I returned to the living room thumbing through the *Yellow Pages* until I located Psychologists. This time Bob sounded frantic. "What are you looking for?"

I traced the listings with my index finger until one name caught my eye, "An omen!" I shouted as I pointed to "Adler" the name of the renowned psychologist, Alfred Adler. My sense of hopelessness disappeared as I dialed the telephone number. I was about to hang up on the fourth ring when a voice answered. I was delighted to reach a human being instead of an answering machine. Dr. Adler forwarded calls home on Sunday in case of an emergency.

I explained that we were at the end of the proverbial rope and desperately needed help. He graciously suggested we see him in his home that afternoon. From the moment his broad smile greeted us I knew we were in capable hands.

"Please come in and makes yourselves comfortable. I hope you didn't have trouble finding the house."

"No, no trouble," Bob and I responded in unison.

We were ushered in to a well-appointed living room where we gravitated toward opposite ends of a "love seat." Dr. Adler positioned himself in the high-backed chair across from us.

"Well, what brings you here today?"

There was an uncomfortable pause during which Bob and I glanced at each other, but neither of us dared to speak. I was afraid once the floodgates opened we would drown if we spoke.

Dr. Adler's voice jolted me back to the moment. "On the phone, you said you desperately needed help." Bob remained silent. It was up to me to take the initiative, to reveal our marriage was a disastrous mess and we did not have a clue how to fix it.

"I don't know where to begin," I said. "There are so many things wrong. Our marriage is falling apart. We're falling apart."

"Take a moment to think about the one incident that prompted you to call today."

Dr. Adler looked directly at Bob. "Either of you may answer the question."

"We only have a marriage for half of each year. The rest of the time Bob doesn't function."

"Do you mean in the bedroom?"

My face flushed. "I didn't mean it in that way—well that too, but what I meant was—in every other way. He becomes a non-person. The rest of the time—well, there are other issues." I was reluctant to continue. I already felt like a traitor.

"Bob, is there something you care to add to what Lee has already said?"

No response.

"Well then—I feel we've made a good start here. Why don't you call me in my office tomorrow and we can arrange an appointment that is convenient for both of you."

Bob and I nodded. When we rose to leave I feared my life would be forever altered, but I looked forward to shedding the last vestiges of this painful existence.

After our initial meeting we continued to see Dr. Adler on a regular basis. At first it was slow-going. I was anxious to discuss pertinent issues which led us to reach out for help—while Bob spent most of the time with two fingers placed across his lips.

At home, Bob's erratic behavior escalated to the point where I never knew what to anticipate. My greatest fear was that he would place a pillow over my face while I slept.

Meaning you could no longer sleep in the same room with him, said Ms. Freud.

During the next session with Dr. Adler I explained that I would feel more comfortable sleeping in Michelle's old room. Bob became visibly upset and vehemently disapproved of any decision to abandon him.

He offered an alternate plan. With Michelle out of the house he wanted to convert her bedroom into a TV room with two recliners and a television set. I had once suggested we purchase a convertible couch to put in that room, or the living room, just in case anyone wanted to sleep over.

My suggestion caused a roaring declaration: "No one is going to sleep in my living room!"

Dr. Adler agreed with my suggestion that I move in to the other bedroom. The arrangement would offer a respite from each other— and also provide a quiet place to complete my schoolwork. At the same time, Dr. Adler suggested Bob consider taking a diagnostic test which would help assess information provided by Bob during therapy.

At first Bob bristled, and Dr. Adler quickly explained that the "The Minnesota Multiphasic Personality Inventory (MMPI) used clinical scales designed to identify personality disorders and psychopathology listed in the *Diagnostic Statistical Manual of Mental Disorders (DSM)*."

Despite Dr. Adler's professional tone Bob burst out laughing. "Sounds like a mouthful of mumbo-jumbo to me Doc, but if it will make you and Lee happy you can test all you want."

That evening I moved into my new sleeping quarters—where I made certain to depress the push-button lock before going to sleep—followed later with being roused by a muffled sound outside the door.

"Bob is that you?"

No response.

"Bob is that you out there!" I yelled.

I peered into the hallway just in time to see Bob's bedroom door close.

The following morning tiny paint chips stuck to my bare feet as I stumbled toward the bathroom. At first I couldn't understand the source. I was certain the floor was clear before I went to sleep.

After I recalled the strange noise I heard in the night I inspected the door—and while checking the lock for scratches. I was horrified to find paint missing from the hinge pins.

Bob had attempted to remove the door while I slept.

I gathered the paint fragments and presented them to Bob during breakfast. "Do you have any idea where these came from? They were on the floor in front of my bedroom door."

Bob turned the chips over in his hand and shrugged his shoulders.

"No idea," he replied, staring into his coffee mug.

It was obvious that just locking my door would not be enough of a deterrent. I needed to take more drastic precautionary measures. From then on I pushed the nightstand and a portable television set against the door each night, wrapped the electrical cord around the doorknob and pulled it through a handle before knotting it in place.

Mixed with fear and anger was my frustration in not understanding how Bob expected me to react. He insisted I leave my door unlocked at night. He refused to understand that I locked it because he was out of control. Ironically there were times he admitted being out of control.

Here we were—still engaged in a normal relationship—when our life was anything but normal.

CHAPTER THIRTEEN

During our marriage Bob worked at a succession of jobs. He was "gung ho" at the beginning, but eventually would feel the need to move on and make more money. His most recent job was only a short distance from the house. The suits and ties he wore previously were replaced with casual attire. He developed new computer applications for which he received the praise and admiration of co-workers—and he appeared calmer and happier than ever before.

Thus I was shocked to learn a fork-lift had run over Bob's foot at work. I found it hard to believe that he didn't hear the fork-lift beeping when it backed up, or that the operator didn't see him in the side-view mirrors. Given Bob's generally erratic behavior, I also wondered if the accident was a result of a senseless game, or an act of revenge.

The doctors avoided surgery by meticulously picking out tiny bone fragments from his mangled toes. Bob was released from the hospital in a hard cast up to his calf and crutches for mobility. He was fortunate none of his toes had to be amputated, but after the cast was removed he had difficulty flexing the injured foot.

During the time Bob was on disability he ran me ragged and ordered me around as if I were his servant. When I wasn't chauffeuring him or pushing his wheelchair I was fending off his sexual advances.

He was oblivious to the welts the cast inflicted as he thrashed about during bouts of intimacy.

Eventually Bob became restless at work and once again expressed a need to earn more money. He accepted a position as a manufacturer's representative which offered greater financial potential.

Bob was with the new company only a short time before he griped about how difficult it was to comply with requirements of this new job. His boss called early in the morning while we were still in bed. There were also meetings that cut in to his selling time and sales quotas were difficult to meet.

Papers and unopened envelopes were strewn across the desktop in his basement office. The piles grew higher and his trips up and down the stairs became more frequent, the thumping of his feet more urgent. I surmised that he was constantly searching for something he could not find, but he usually returned empty-handed muttering obscenities.

Against my better judgment I offered to help him organize that paperwork. At first he refused, and then relented. When I attempted to make sense of the mess I suddenly then saw the reality of Bob—the disorganization was a literal reflection of his disordered mind. He was unable to respond to the simplest question and eventually his frustration turned to anger—which of course he vented by blasting me with expletives.

That was the last time I volunteered to help.

And despite Bob's constant complaining he became one of the firm's top salesmen. His boss invited us to join him and another top-producer for a weekend at a casino resort in Atlantic City. The other two couples would share a suite with a jacuzzi. From the moment Bob learned we would occupy a standard room in a wing of the hotel undergoing renovation I sensed his displeasure.

When we arrived at the hotel, bustling workmen were everywhere. After we were forced to detour around an overflowing trash can placed under the leaking ceiling, I was certain Bob was close to exploding. The elevator door opened on our floor and we stepped into a mish-mash of new and old rolled carpets, piles of wallpaper and buckets of paste. Apparently the renovation was not limited to the lobby.

I held my breath as Bob slowly opened the door to our room. I was relieved to find new carpeting and freshly painted walls. He circled the room, pulled out drawers, yanked drapes back and forth and checked to see if the television and air-conditioner operated properly.

He then spun around as if looking for any excuse to release the rage building since we arrived. He quickly moved toward the closet and repeatedly slid the doors back and forth until one door jumped off the track. He sprinted to the phone on the bedside table and dialed his boss' room number. I was petrified as I braced myself for the tirade to come.

"Who the hell do you think I am!" he yelled. "You and Murray have a suite and I have to stay in a broken down hell-hole?"

Before he could respond, Bob described the leak in the lobby and the broken closet in a language so colorful it would have made a longshoreman blush. "You're sorry? You should be sorry!" He slammed down the phone and directed his wrath toward me. I cowered in the corner as I prayed he would not become violent.

"Can you believe it? My boss had the nerve to say he's sorry. There's no other room available so we're stuck in this shit-hole for the weekend!" I should have kept my mouth shut, but I thought I would help by suggesting he call maintenance to report the closet door.

"The door," he bellowed. "You think this is about the fucking door? I don't like being treated like a second-class citizen," Bob snarled. This time I kept my mouth shut. Bob pushed past me and with one hand on either side of the disengaged door, bounced it several times until it jumped back on the track. "There! I fixed the God-damned door!"

Shortly after we returned home I foolishly inquired why Bob was sitting on the couch pouting. He often made hurtful remarks, but nothing compared with his out-of-left field accusation that I had prevented him from becoming a real father.

"I'm angry because you had your tubes tied."

"I had my tubes tied?" I repeated incredulously. "We agreed that I would have my tubes tied after my gynecologist suggested I stop taking birth control pills."

It wouldn't have made a difference if I reminded Bob we both agreed not to have a child together—or that he had been delighted at the prospect of my becoming a sex-machine. He would claim he had no recollection of our conversation.

"If you felt so strongly about wanting a child of your own you should have accepted the offer I made before we were married, to be free-to go forth and multiply." At first Bob hesitated as if he were searching for the right words.

"You know that's not what I want," he whispered.

I retreated to my bedroom leaving him sitting on the couch, sulking.

Bob seemed unusually cheerful when he returned home from work the next day. He had learned that sales reps would soon attend a trade show in Atlanta, Georgia. However, and instead of sitting down to dinner, he went upstairs to pack for the trip.

Packing, despite not leaving for two more weeks, said Ms. Freud.

Before he did leave two weeks later I advised him to eat on a regular schedule and watch his sugar intake. I suggested he keep the Diabanese for his diabetes and Xanax to help with day-to-day stress to himself. I felt like a mother talking to her child before sending him off to summer camp.

Bob nodded.

And you wondered if he resented your intrusion, said
Ms. Freud, and would deliberately disregard your advice.

Concerned about his loss of income during the trade show week, Bob was calling on as many customers as possible before leaving for Atlanta.

He also needed cash for the trip, but was to busy to go to the bank himself, and so asked me to deposit a portion of his commission check and request the balance in cash. After I repeated his instructions to the teller she checked the signature cards. She scrutinized one signature card in particular before heading toward the bank manager's glass-enclosed cubicle.

The transaction seemed simple enough, but something's
wrong, said Ms. Freud.

I watched as she handed the signature card to the official looking gentlemen while leaning down to whisper in his ear. My heart pounded. The manager waved me into his office.

"Miss O'Brien informed me you want to cash a check against your husband's account?"

"Yes—is there a problem?" I asked rhetorically, knowing full well there must be one hell of a problem or I would not be sitting in his office.

"Are you aware your name is not listed on this account?" the manager continued.

Did a piano just fall on you, queried Ms. Freud?

I was momentarily dazed. From across the desk I could see Bob's lone signature on the card. "That's impossible," I sputtered. "I'm sure I signed a signature card at this bank."

"And so you did," the officer assured me. He deftly pulled a second card from beneath the first one, reminding me of a magician hoping to impress with sleight-of-hand.

"I don't understand," I managed.

"You… and… your… husband… have… a… joint… checking account." He enunciated each word as if speaking to an idiot. "I'm afraid the other account," waiving the signature card in my face, "is only in your husband's name."

Once again he enunciated to the idiot sitting across from him. "Do…you…understand?"

"I get it! I get it!" I said, losing my composure.

"I'm very sorry," he apologized handing back the check and deposit slip. I felt humiliated as he reached out to shake my hand. I was fit to kill and Bob was lucky I calmed down before he arrived home.

"Hey, did you get to the bank?" he called out as he entered the kitchen.

"Did I get to the bank? You bet your ass I did!"

"What kind of an answer is that? Did you cash the check or didn't you?"

After I gave him a run-down of the events and explained how mortified I felt, His only concern was the check.

"What happened to the God-damn check?"

"They gave it back!"

"I suppose I'll have to go to the bank tomorrow."

"That's it? That's all you have to say?"

"What do you want me to say, that you're making a mountain out of a mole hill?"

"You're the one with the secret bank account," I said, poking him in the chest for emphasis.

"What secret bank account? It's a stinking little account I use to cash my commission checks. Then I take money out and deposit it in our checking account."

I knew something was fishy, but I wasn't sure what. Clearly Bob didn't think there was anything wrong with the way he handled our finances when clearly and virtually everything was wrong.

CHAPTER FOURTEEN

I appreciated the time alone during Bob's trade show absence. The house was unusually peaceful and I relaxed. Late one evening I answered the phone expecting to hear Bob's voice. Instead I recognized his boss Lou's frantic tone.

Lou did his best to explain that Bob had experienced a seizure at the trade show, and in turn had become violent when at the hospital—followed by now being in the hospital's psychiatric ward.

Lou was clearly uncomfortable and concerned about Bob's state of mind. He wanted to know if I had any idea what caused him to "go off." I swore nothing like that had ever happened before.

He was in a quandary about what to do if Bob called the hotel in the middle of the night and demanded somebody come to get him. I was sure Lou thought it strange when I suggested he request the hotel operator put a "Do Not Disturb" on his phone line. I promised to get back to him after speaking with the admitting doctor. Lou breathed a sigh of relief, grateful that I would follow up about Bob.

Before making the call to Atlanta I sat for a long time trying to sort out the events of the last couple of days.

1. My mentally ill husband leaves on a business trip, and I am secretly delighted that he is away.

2. I can sleep without barricading my bedroom door.

3. After I am notified he has experienced a medical emergency I cannot bring myself to make the phone call I know must be made.

Must be made, mused Ms. Freud.

I dialed the telephone number Lou had given me and was eventually connected with the psychiatric nurse familiar with Bob's case. Once I identified myself as Bob's wife, Nurse Andrew filled me in.

Bob had experienced a grand mal seizure that was so intense it nearly severed his tongue.

"Fortunately the seizure was of short duration, but your husband sustained a minor concussion in addition to some blood loss from the trauma to his mouth. The information gathered at the scene and the subsequent blood tests indicated your husband had been drinking heavily the night before. In the morning his co-workers had difficulty rousing him. Bob insisted on skipping breakfast and did not take his diabetes medication."

"These events contributed to your husband's seizure," Nurse Andrew went on to explain, adding: "When your husband learned he would be staying in the hospital overnight, he became abusive to the EMS personnel, the hospital staff and his boss. He had to be restrained and a psychiatric consultation was ordered. Once your husband's medical condition was stabilized he was transferred to the psych unit for observation." Andrew assured me Bob was sedated and resting peacefully.

I had been crying the entire time Andrew was talking. Visualizing Bob in restraints tore at my heart. I imagined him reliving his experience as a teenager, confined to a psychiatric hospital, terrified. When Andrew questioned me about Bob's medical and psychiatric history I held nothing back. I told him about Bob's previous hospital commitment, his recent behavior and the need to secure my bedroom door at night. Andrew and I agreed this would be an ideal time for Bob to be evaluated by a neurologist.

I asked Andrew if I should fly down. He assured me everything that could be done would be done and I should get a good night's sleep and not worry. He provided a pager number and told me to call anytime. As soon as test results became available, or if additional information was required, someone would be in touch, he said.

I came away, wishfully thinking perhaps in my certainty that a brain abnormality would help explain Bob's behavior.

Otherwise he's just plain crazy, said Ms. Freud.

I called Lou and assured him Bob was in good hands.

"It must have been frightening for you to witness Bob's seizure," I offered.

"You can't imagine how scared and helpless we felt when out of nowhere," Lou said, and immediately apologized. "I'm sorry Lee—you really don't want to hear the gory details—do you?"

"It's all right Lou, go ahead. You can say whatever you want. I think it would be good for both of us to talk about it."

Lou hesitated for a moment as if deciding just how much information to reveal.

"Well—I was just standing around talking with the other salesmen until Bob walked over to join us. He looked pale and was perspiring profusely. Before anyone had a chance to ask what was wrong he tried to grab my arm before he toppled over. Bob's limbs were flailing, his head banged against the floor and there was blood everywhere. It was horrible—just horrible. Thank God the EMS arrived quickly."

"Do you think I should be there with Bob? I'll fly down if you say so."

"It's not necessary. I'll bring our boy home in a couple of days after the trade show closes."

"I can't thank you enough. I know you'll bring him home safe and sound. Have a good night, Lou."

"Good night, Lee. Don't worry, he'll be all right."

Ms. Freud grimaced: *That's what you think, Lou.*

Zombie-like, I stumbled through the rest of the day and hurried home from work hoping to find a message from Andrew. I did not know whether to feel concerned or relieved after I heard the recording announce, "You have no new messages."

I had an hour before evening classes; I paged Andrew and he had nothing new to report. The neurologist was still waiting for MRI results. Andrew suggested I call the following day and ask for Dr. Patterson. All the responsibilities as Bob's caregiver were temporarily lifted. I felt elated. Later that night with my bedroom door wide open, I slept without fear for the first time in a long while.

Dr. Patterson explained that the test results were unremarkable; there were no visible abnormalities. Bob's mental illness could be treated with a combination of therapy and psychotropic drugs. After I thanked the doctor, a grey cloud of fear descended as I dreaded the thought of dealing with Bob if he returned home in a foul mood.

When I heard a car screech to a halt outside the house followed by a loud thud, I assumed I would have the opportunity to speak to the person who dropped Bob off.

Before reaching the door I heard a car accelerate, followed by finding Bob all alone on the porch, dumped like yesterday's trash.

Face a lifeless mask, at first glance he resembled a mannequin. And when he bent down to pick up an overturned suitcase I was shocked at his lack of coordination. He appeared to have had a stroke or at the least be heavily medicated. Flaccid arms dangled and wobbly legs flopped like freshly caught fish struggling for a last desperate breath.

Decision time, said Ms. Freud.

I was uncertain if I should call 9-1-1 or drive Bob to the emergency room. I cautiously led him into the living room where he remained standing until I instructed him to sit down.

I thought it best to treat him like the psych patient he was and do an intake to determine if he was oriented to time and place. When I asked him if he knew where he was and to name the day of the week he stared at me incredulously. His throat emitted an eerie sound, an unsuccessful attempt at laughter—and despite a vacant look, he answered my questions correctly.

I asked if he felt hungry and if he wanted to go to his favorite restaurant for a hamburger. He became more alert at the mention of food, but when I asked him to name the restaurant he responded, "You know—you know, the one." He was unable to remember.

After I suggested we stop at the Emergency Room on the way, he became agitated and refused to leave the house. I had to promise we would proceed directly to the restaurant; only then would he budge.

Bob experienced some difficulty getting in and out of the car, but did not have a problem chewing or swallowing food. By the time we returned home and retired to separate bedrooms we were emotionally drained.

"Aren't you late for work?" he growled the next morning.

"How would it look if I left you alone and while I was at work you stumbled down the stairs and broke your neck?" I asked, half joking.

I reached for Bob's hand. His muscle-tone was still not what it should have been.

I called his internist; Dr. Russell recommended I drive him to the ER. When I reiterated that he refused to go to the hospital Dr. Russell reluctantly agreed to see Bob in his office—if I could get him there.

After I hung up I could see from Bob's expression that he would continue to be obstinate. Before he had a chance to protest I proposed two choices: either the ER or the doctor's office. He angrily opted for the latter.

After examining Bob, Dr. Russell asked if I brought the name of the attending physician in Atlanta. Fortunately, I remembered to put that information into my handbag.

Dr. Russell made the call from a wall phone and allowed us to hear his portion of the conversation. After inquiring about Bob's recent hospitalization, he shook his head in disbelief.

"You gave him how much Librium? You give that much to an elephant!"

After slamming the phone he declared, "Bob is fine. He was prescribed too much Librium. We have to wean him off the drug by gradually reducing the dosage. I'll write him a prescription."

The following evening found us with long-time friends Jack and Arlene. They called to ask if we were in the mood for Spanish food and suggested we join them.

Arlene was anxious to know how everything was between Bob and you, opined Ms. Freud.

After I gave Arlene a brief synopsis I asked if they still wanted us to join them for dinner. Arlene assured me they were familiar with Bob's "kooky" behavior and we agreed on a time to pick us up. Bob perked up when I told him we were going out with our two oldest and dearest friends.

The next day I tried to stay out of Bob's way and avoid conversation that would possibly set him off. During the afternoon I was relieved when he agreed to lie down for a nap. On the way to the restaurant Bob insisted Jack change lanes, slow down or watch out for yellow traffic signals. Jack ignored him while Arlene tried unsuccessfully to engage Bob in conversation.

Hope you haven't made an error in judgment, said Ms. Freud.

I was thankful we did not have a long wait before being seated. After the menus were distributed our drink order was taken. When the waiter returned, Arlene and Jack were still pondering the menu.

"You're keeping the waiter waiting!" Bob exclaimed. "Let's go! Let's go! Give him your order already. Lee ordered. I ordered. What's taking you so long?"

Arlene and Jack looked stunned, followed by Arlene's sarcasm. "That's what waiters do Bob—they wait."

"I'm tired of waiting. I want to eat," Bob argued.

When Bob's entrée arrived, he angrily announced, "I didn't order this crap!" He then began spearing food with his fork and flinging it onto our plates. Just at that moment a strolling guitarist approached our table. Bob reached into his pocket, thrust a $10 bill at him and demanded he leave.

Arlene was angry. "Why did you do that Bob? Maybe somebody else wants to hear him play?"

Bob leaped up, threw several $20 bills on the table and announced, "I don't have to take this!" He then stormed out of the restaurant.

Jack's eyes grew wide. Arlene's mouth literally fell open.

I remained calm, gathered up the money Bob had scattered about and put my feet up on the seat he had vacated. I took a long sip of wine.

"There's plenty of money here," I announced. "Let's relax and enjoy the rest of our dinner." Jerry agonized over how Bob would get

77

home, but I wasn't the least bit concerned. "I don't know and I don't care. That's his problem, not mine."

After Jack and Arlene drove me home I found Bob sitting on the couch watching television. As if nothing unusual had happened earlier that evening, he inquired, "Did you have a nice time?"

"I had a lovely time—after you left," I replied.

Quickly I ascended the stairs to my sanctuary.

And sometime later you were deep in thought as you sorted the soiled clothing, said Ms. Freud. Wait, what's this as you lifted a pair of Bob's briefs and pulled a course, black hair from the soft fabric. The texture and color were unlike Bob's or your hair—proof he was screwing around.

I carefully wrapped the evidence in a tissue and placed it an envelope in my handbag. I confronted Bob in Dr. Adler's office. But as I slowly unfolded the tissue, the hair had mysteriously disappeared.

Bob refused to admit he had looked through your bag and thrown the hair away, Ms. Freud sighed.

Just like I had been refusing for years to see the *Big Lie.*

CHAPTER FIFTEEN

I never realized how multi-faceted our marital discord was until I compiled a list of the issues facing us. The resulting manifesto I presented to Bob:

1. **Privacy And Space:** I finally have a place of my own where, and if I choose, I can read, watch television or simply be alone. I can enjoy a night or a Saturday to myself without you asking to join me.

2. **Money:** You don't like it when I question you about money. You can't be trusted. I have to look out for myself. I have no intention of becoming a bag lady or relying on charity. You resent the fact that I have a bank account. If I drop dead tomorrow why shouldn't my daughter have something from her mother? What is wrong with that? Over the years my account has been routinely depleted in order to finance our vacations, my car, wedding expenses and home furnishings. I always thought I was doing the right thing by contributing to our finances, but you never appreciated my efforts. I'm finally doing something for me just like you did when you had your deck built. You cut food money to the bone. If money for food is scarce, money for going out is too. From now on we share these expenses. The summer presents additional problems. My Silver Gull Beach Club membership costs me $600. You buy guest passes for yourself and strut around acting like a king. If we invite a guest on the weekend, I pay for them. If you want to continue your masquerade, pay for

your own membership. I want the home equity loan paid up and cancelled. I am equally responsible for the $50,000. It is not a sound idea to keep such a large line of credit open.

3. **Winter:** I am through putting up with your withdrawal each winter. If you can't get your act together during that time of year then I'll do what's necessary for me to survive.

4. **Opinions:** I no longer offer my opinion. You complain that I don't answer you fast enough and you misunderstand what I say or get upset if I disagree with you. I'm tired of hearing that I always have to have my own way when it is you who act like a spoiled child and must have your own way. I don't want to argue about everything. Nothing is that important to me. Unlike you, after I give my opinion I have learned not to give two shits about the outcome.

5. **Infidelity**: I don't know if I can ever trust you again. Do I have to start using condoms with my own husband (I have been advised to do so). If you need diversions outside our marriage or kinky sex, be honest and admit it. And unless you are sure you can keep your dick in your pants don't even consider a future with me.

6. **Security/Insurance**: Since you didn't see fit to buy mortgage insurance or life insurance—and also didn't think it important to have a will—you seem to think you're going to live forever. What about a disability policy? If you're unable to work all plans and money fly out the window.

Despite that my manifesto elicited zero comment from Bob we continued to work on our marriage. After we discussed Bob's hospitalization in Georgia and his subsequent acting out with Jack and Arlene—and others, Dr. Adler recommended individual counseling in addition to marriage counseling.

During my session I questioned if psychotropic drugs would make a difference in Bob's behavior. Dr. Adler believed Bob would benefit from such drugs, but not without embracing them as part of an overall therapy plan.

He went on to explain there are mental disorders that overlap, making an accurate diagnosis difficult. Some people exhibit extremes of elated or depressed mood and may suffer for years before properly diagnosed with manic-depression (bipolar) disorder. It is an illness that must be managed throughout a person's life. Many individuals with bipolar disorder often experience a pattern of fall depressions and spring-summer hypomania, termed seasonal affective disorder (SAD). The description certainly matched Bob's symptoms.

I was hopeful Dr. Adler would steer him in the right direction. Eventually he convinced Bob to be evaluated by Dr. Perry, a psycho-pharmacologist who was the head of psychiatry at a local hospital. He agreed to see Bob as a private patient if Bob would agree to one year of supervised treatment.

That resulted in Bob beginning to take Lithium, commonly prescribed for manic-depression (bipolar disorder). I noticed subtle changes in his behavior and he experienced less mood cycling. I prayed this was the beginning of the stable relationship we craved so desperately.

And then along came the mood monster, said Ms. Freud.

One Sunday Bob came stomping up the stairs from his basement office.

"I don't like the way I feel," he announced.

"What's the matter? Are you sick?"

"I'm not me; I'm fatigued, my stomach is a mess and I'm just tired of feeling like crap all the time. I don't want to take the medication."

I insisted he call his psychiatrist and repeat what he had just told me.

"It's Sunday. I don't want to bother Dr. Perry and he's probably not in anyway," Bob argued.

"I'm sure his service will pick up."

I insisted he make the call. After he stomped past me I heard his muffled voice from the next room. He reappeared and announced smugly, "Dr. Perry told me I don't have to take the medication if I don't want to."

"That's it? That's all he said?"

"Oh yeah, he wants to see me tomorrow after work."

The next evening Bob returned home with a "do not approach" expression. He remained withdrawn for the balance of the evening. It was unnecessary for me to ask what had transpired during his appointment with Dr. Perry; his face said it all. I was certain he told Bob that if he refused to take Lithium, treatment could not continue.

Ms. Freud muttered: And no matter how hopeless your marriage seemed, you and mood monster continued to socialize with friends from your remarried organization.

The other remarried couples in fact never suspected our marriage was in trouble. Astoundingly, Bob and I were held up as role models:

1. No problems with ex-spouses.
2. Always laughing.
3. Always dancing.

And it was often observed that how we moved on the dance floor suggested how compatible we were in bed.

Which fed the all-important ego, smirked Ms. Freud.

We continued to socialize at "house-warming" parties after several couples moved to Staten Island. And at Barry and Diane's new home we were introduced to that couple's friend—Madam Marion.

Diane asked the group who wanted Marion to read Tarot cards. At first everybody was skeptical, snickering and elbowing each other before settling down. Marion herself then asked who wanted cards read.

And of course Bob volunteered, sighed Ms. Freud.

Marion shuffled and cut the mystical Tarot deck. She carefully placed a spread of colorful cards on the table, face up and began her interpretation.

"This is a time when much is happening. Here are the ups and downs of life." Marion pointed toward the Three of Swords. "Sorrow, heartache, and a time for endings, bitter words have much pain."

A hush descended; the audience was mesmerized.

Marion glanced at the next card and inquired if Bob and I were certain we wanted her to continue.

The full impact of her words had not yet sunken in as mentally we were all still in parlor trick mode.

Besides, Marion couldn't possibly know your marriage was in shambles, crooned Ms. Freud.

We encouraged her to continue.

The next card was the Five of Swords. "This is a time of tension and unpleasantness." Once again, Marion asked if she should continue. We assured her we were comfortable with her reading. "There is a desire to escape." She hesitated for a moment and lowered her voice. "Cruel words are in the air. Watch out for underhanded actions."

The final card was the Eight of Cups. "There is a decline of interest; life is without meaning. It is time to look for something more meaningful." Marion was on the verge of tears. "I'm so sorry," she apologized. "I had no idea my reading would reveal so much. I am so, so, sorry."

Bob and I were stunned by Marion's insightful interpretation. When we glanced around our gaze was met with bewilderment, until Diane dared to inquire.

"Is it true? Is what Marion said really true?"

Bob and I acknowledged that Marion had indeed spoken the truth. Not having to hide our secret any longer was a welcome relief.

PART THREE

**HOLD
TIGHT**

CHAPTER SIXTEEN

Bob had been trying to arrange a dinner appointment with his cousins Irene and Gary. He fumed for hours after a previous unsuccessful attempt to agree on a date. Irene and Gary did not have a clue our marriage was disintegrating and I did not wish to share the sordid details with more people than necessary. Nonetheless, Bob flew into a rage when I suggested he make an excuse for why I would not be joining them.

And he was clueless that his anger was a major part of the problem, sighed Ms. Freud.

Neither of us was ready to make a life altering decision about a future together. With Dr. Adler's guidance we agreed on an arrangement that allowed for more independence. We were encouraged to think clearly about what we wanted for ourselves, and needed from each other. We continued to sleep in separate bedrooms and share weekend expenses.

This is why you left a note on the kitchen table, said Ms. Freud, before going to bed.

"I owe you approximately $16 for our Dutch Treat lunch and dinner. Do you want me to go shopping tomorrow? You can reimburse me for your share in the evening."

Bob barely glanced at the note before leaving the next day. I returned home at 6 p.m., gave him the $16 I owed and explained that I would have stopped to pick up something for dinner if he had responded to my note.

"You and your notes, I'm sick and tired of notes! I deal with notes all damn day, messages from receptionists, memos from my boss. I'm drowning in notes! You know what you can do with your God-damn notes?"

His anger had reached volcanic proportions. I wasn't sure what I dreaded the most, the silence in between anticipating his outburst or the actual eruption.

The next morning, Bob entered the kitchen speaking in rapid staccato. "I didn't know you were up already—good morning—it looks like it's going to be a scorcher today—the newspaper is outside—are you going to the beach club—are you coming home for dinner—have a nice day."

I waited for a lull before responding. "You never answer any of my questions. Now you expect me to answer yours?"

"Like I said, have a nice day."

"I intend to."

Following Bob's announcement that "I can't go on wasting my life indefinitely." Dr. Adler suggested we decide on a time-frame for consulting a divorce lawyer—and we agreed to wait until fall.

The next day I was stunned by Bob's exceptionally cheery "Good morning" followed by, "In the next week or two make up a list of what you want to take when you leave."

"When I leave?" I asked, in disbelief. "Isn't it, if I leave? Don't you remember what we discussed with Dr. Adler?"

It was pointless to continue. I started to walk away. Bob besieged me to stay and explain our agreement. I suggested he call Dr. Adler for clarification. I would not ride the merry-go-round this day.

Later I overheard a conversation. "So you're off for the whole summer—you lucky dog." The man sounded genuinely happy for his friend.

You always had to defend your time off to Bob, said Ms. Freud.

He resented that I was off during the summer while he had to work. Employment in the public school system came with perks: an annualized salary with an optional summer session and generous medical benefits. In addition to my full-time job I attended college two nights a week. I deserved the summer off.

I was on my way out of the door when Bob asked, "Will you be home this evening?"

"You're asking questions again without offering any information. Are you coming home for dinner?" I inquired.

"I'm on my way to New Jersey for my monthly sales meeting with the men and you're going to make me late." Bob sounded exasperated.

"And will you be home for dinner?" I repeated.

His face twisted into a grotesque mask as spittle oozed from the corners of his mouth.

"I won't be home for dinner!" he roared.

"Then why don't you just say so? Do you think I obtain information by osmosis?"

Bob placed two fingers across his lips to signal the conversation had ended. The gesture was a reminder that I had just talked to a wall.

Bob left for work.

Or so he said, smirked Ms. Freud.

I was becoming increasingly suspicious of his every move.

When I looked in the green metal box in our bedroom closet, the checkbook for the home equity loan was missing. The bankbooks were replaced with a note—something about the bankbooks being updated.

I was concerned Bob would transfer the accounts to other banking instruments. When I asked him about the missing items all hell broke loose. He acknowledged that he had hidden the check book for the loan because he was responsible for it and promised to return the other bank books after the updates.

It was out of character for Bob to allow anything that important to be left out of his hands for any length of time. He wanted to know why I really looked in the metal box, and followed that with an accusation that I was planning to cash in the bankbooks.

"I only wanted to check the ownership and the names of the banks."

"I know you're going to take me to the cleaners—I just know it," he wailed.

One evening I found Bob reading personal papers I foolishly left out on my dresser. When I questioned why he was in my room his excuse was about wanting to see how my jumbo jig-saw puzzle was progressing.

I no longer had the patience or energy to make every item an incident—but my friend Evelyn's words echoed loudly within:

"He's counting on wearing you down. He knows you don't want to deal with his shit-fits. The longer you wait to end this thing the more ways he'll find to screw you over."

CHAPTER SEVENTEEN

Our in-house separation was unrealistic and filled with tension.

Bob still looked forward to dinner—and yet complained about the limited menu.

What did he expect if he never answered your questions about whether or not to go shopping, queried Ms. Freud?

If there was spaghetti in the pantry, I prepared dinner. I would retire to my room after cleaning up the kitchen.

Whenever Bob had trouble remembering, I considered the possibility his memory was affected by the electro-shock therapy he received as a young man

Or maybe a traumatic brain injury at birth, asked Ms. Freud?

Bea delighted in repeating the story about Bob's forceps delivery and how the depressions on either side of his head were still noticeable days after she gave birth. Working with the special needs population made me keenly aware of brain damage caused during childbirth.

Bob was napping when I returned home one evening and didn't awaken until it was time for dinner. We ate leftovers and watched a video. This rare interlude of normalcy was interrupted by a phone call from his cousin thanking him for a flower delivery.

You knew nothing about this, sighed Ms. Freud, but this wasn't the first time your name was omitted from a gift card.

My friend Sandy recommended I read *When Madness Comes Home* after I confided my frustration about Bob's failing memory. The book referred to a fugue state where a person really doesn't recall what's said, done or even heard.

One evening, Bob initiated a conversation about feelings, communication and acknowledging responsibility. This was the first time we had ever discussed these issues. He informed me he was finally at a place in his therapy where he finished dealing with his anger and was ready to move on.

But you were doubtful, said Ms. Freud.

We discussed the upcoming holiday weekend and agreed to spend the Fourth of July together. We planned driving to a new shopping mall in New Jersey. Bob agreed when I suggested we have breakfast at home in order to get an early start.

When I awoke to a glorious July Fourth morning Bob was seated in the kitchen waiting for me while impatiently tapping his fingers on the table.

"Would like to eat breakfast out?" he asked.

"I thought we agreed to eat at home."

"I changed my mind. We can stop on the way and eat breakfast at Perkins."

Bob departed for the bathroom where his rambling was audible through the closed door. When he emerged, he wanted to know where I felt like eating.

"We already decided on Perkins."

"We decided?"

"It's all right with me if you don't want to go to Perkins," I replied. By that time, I was ready to scream.

"Perkins is fine!" Bob angrily replied.

It was obvious, nothing was fine. The promise of a sinfully deli-cious breakfast clouded my judgment and I followed him out the door.

Like a lamb to slaughter, sighed Ms. Freud.

When we arrived Bob instructed me to go inside and give the hostess our name so we would not have to wait "17 hours." After breakfast we continued without further discussion. At each highway sign he pulled over to the side of the road, lit a cigarette and consulted the map. He repeatedly folded and unfolded the map in various config-urations, all the while cursing under his breath. He was completely disoriented and did not have a clue where the shopping center was located and I dreaded the thought of becoming the driver.

Suddenly Bob was pounding the steering wheel. "I don't know where the hell we are! I'm lost!" Before I could respond, he contin-ued, "I should have eaten breakfast sooner. We should have studied the map before we left."

I had to stifle the impulse to lecture him about assuming responsibility and preparing in advance. I did not relish taking on the job of pathfinder and caregiver, but I did not have a choice. I insisted Bob move over and allow me to drive.

"Here—you read the map. See if you can do any better," he said, thrusting the crumpled map toward me.

After I pulled in to a gas station Bob snarled, "Do you want to ask for directions or should I?" Before I could answer he bounded out of the car.

As soon as he was out of sight, my tears freely flowed. "What the hell are you crying for?" he asked upon returning.

A question you could not begin to answer, said Ms. Freud.

We continued with Bob reciting the information he received at the gas station. Upon arriving I pulled in to the first available space and exited, but after a few steps I sensed Bob was not behind me.

I turned to see his head bobbing around and assumed he had knocked off the rear-view mirror. He had done the same thing the last time he obsessed over the best way to place the cardboard sunvisor across the dashboard.

What difference does it make if the car was 100 degrees or 110 degrees—hot is hot, said Ms. Freud.

I sat on the stone perimeter, waiting, swinging my legs and anticipating the worst. I was qualified to work in a mental institution. I already lived in one and now I was spending the day with one of my charges.

My thoughts were interrupted as Bob approached and informed me, "Somewhere between giving you the money for the toll and asking for directions, I lost my money clip." I chastised him for not putting his money in a better place, especially after he once commented that the shorts he was wearing had shallow pockets.

Bob lashed out, "You make me angry! You cause me aggravation!" I looked toward heaven and tried not to bite off the tip of my tongue. It would have been futile to respond. I suggested we go our separate ways and meet in the food court in two hours. Bob was not happy with the plan, but by then I did not give a damn how he felt. When we met later, I was relaxed and I hoped Bob would be too.

Wrong, said Ms. Freud.

"Have you seen all the stores?" I foolishly inquired.

"I didn't see anything. I just walked around and tried to relax," Bob snarled.

"Why don't we meet at the car in about an hour?"

"The mall is open until six o'clock. Take all the time you want," Bob spat through clenched teeth. He took off down the aisle, knocking over chairs along the way and I enjoyed another brief period of freedom.

By the time we arrived home we were both exhausted from the day's events and the long drive through holiday traffic. I announced that I was going upstairs and I would be down in an hour. Bob had been slouched on the couch, pouting, the whole time I was in my room.

In no mood to deal with him, I retreated to my bedroom. Later that night, I placed an itemized list on the kitchen table along with my share of the day's expenses. I felt sorry Bob lost his money clip, but sharing expenses was part of our agreement.

The following evening I looked forward to a night out with my friends. Before I left, Bob had that wild look that usually preceded an emotional outburst.

"You seem angry. Is this left over from yesterday or is it about something new?"

"It's new anger," Bob replied.

"Does it have something to do with me? If it does then we should talk about it before I leave for the evening."

Bob assured me his anger was not about me. He just had a rough day. When I suggested part of his problem may be the inconsistency in the time he takes his anti-anxiety medication, he snarled, "The Xanax has nothing to do with it!"

When I returned home there was no response to my "Hello!" He sat slouched on the couch, glaring.

Hmmm, let's see, said Ms. Freud. He's either mad because you went out for the evening or because you came home—but truth is, you no longer cared why he's mad.

95

I was on my way out when Bob asked what my plans were for dinner. We agreed to take in Chinese food. He insisted we eat in the living room and watch television. I chose the programs as per usual until I made the mistake of asking if there was something special he wanted to watch. Bob informed me he was thinking about it and would let me know when he made up his mind; that was my exit cue. When I told him I was going upstairs he berated me for being too sensitive.

The next evening, Bob handed me the balance of his Silver Gull passes and suggested I use them for my guests. He must have been listening in on my telephone conversation when I confided to Michelle how awkward it was to invite friends on the weekend. I was the member and he paid for the passes, but the club allowed a limited number for each accommodation.

Bob announced he was going to New Jersey on business and would be away several days. He wanted to know my plans for the rest of the month. He suggested we invite the kids over for a barbecue. I reminded him my plans were no longer his concern. He was anxious to arrange something for Eric's birthday.

"If that's what you want, I suggest you extend the invitation and make the arrangements."

"I'll do better than that," he smiled.

Whatever that meant, I did not know nor did I care.

CHAPTER EIGHTEEN

While Bob was in New Jersey I enjoyed being alone. I thought about what it would be like if I were seriously ill and had to take care of myself. I read an article about a man who was receiving chemotherapy. He spent a great deal of time vomiting and cleaning up afterwards. I felt confident I could manage alone.

Bob called to ask if there were any messages for him. He sounded very tranquil, very mellow, very much under the influence of? Of something?

Michelle and I then spent a lovely day together. She invited me back to her house; Eric was not expected home until later. When we stopped to pick up my car, there was a message from Bob: he would be home a day earlier than planned. We left without returning his call.

Eric arrived home just in time to watch the wedding video. Each time Bob appeared on the screen, anger welled up inside me. Instead of enjoying what should have been one of the happiest days of my life his involvement made it one of the saddest.

Bob called to find out what time I was coming home. I planned to leave shortly. He insisted we set a date to celebrate Eric's birthday. When Michelle heard my end of the conversation, she took the telephone receiver and explained that Eric was busy matting and framing photographs for his upcoming exhibit, and could not commit to a specific day to get together.

When I arrived home Bob was in his usual position, slouched on the couch in the dark living room, sulking. Neither of us spoke and

I continued up the stairs to my room.

We looked forward to viewing Eric's photographs in a Manhattan art gallery. The exhibition represented many years of hard work and was a wonderful opportunity for his photographs to be viewed by both critics and art lovers; he would receive the recognition he deserved.

At the same time, Bob and I were anxious to avoid an awkward situation, but we needed to finalize plans for attending the exhibit. I dreaded any discussion on the subject knowing it would not be easy to arrive at an amicable arrangement.

When Bob inquired about the time to leave the house, I visualized the merry-go-round from hell in high gear. My blood-drained knuckles grasped the reins as I held on for dear life. This time I was prepared to ride.

He insisted we leave early. He wanted to have time to stop for something to eat on the way despite knowing food would be served at the gallery. He became visibly annoyed when I suggested we depart at 4 p.m. When I asked what time he had in mind, he responded in a condescending tone that made me want to smack him.

"Why don't I just call you later and maybe then you will have a plan?"

"I expect to be at the beach club most of the afternoon. We need to settle this before I leave. I turned down the kid's offer of a ride so you and I would go together."

"This is getting out of hand. I think the whole thing is becoming problematic. You leave whenever you want and I'll meet you there." Bob insisted.

I arranged to ride to the gallery with Michelle and Eric. Bob arrived an hour later. He shook hands with Eric and his parents, nodded toward Michelle and ignored me. The art gallery was lovely, the wine and hors dóuvres delicious and the piece de résistance,

Eric's incredible photographs, incorporating his signature technique using infrared film.

I had not visited Greenwich Village for a long while. After the gallery filled to capacity I stepped outside. I reflected on how wonderful I felt walking alone, enjoying the quaint shops characteristic of the area. When I returned to the gallery I was surprised to learn Bob had departed soon after I left.

Later that evening a group of family and friends decided on a late supper at a restaurant within walking distance of the gallery. Eric's parents reserved a table in the "garden" on the lower level. When we descended the staircase it was as if we were transported to a vineyard in Italy.

The wooden trellises intertwined with twinkling lights and an incredibly blue faux sky enveloped the ceiling. The conversation was stimulating, the food plentiful and our wine glasses were never empty.

> *You in fact wondered if you had died and gone to heaven, said Ms. Freud, or was this the way it felt when unencumbered by the mood monster?*

Unfortunately all good things come to an end and the marvelous evening ended when Eric drove me home. After I secured my bedroom door I fell into to a deep sleep.

And I dreamed.

Someone mistook me for a teenager. After a male boss reprimanded me, I told him who I was and what I was all about and he shut up.

> *Was that Bob you were telling off, asked Ms. Freud?*

When I awoke I felt certain life would be different next year. In no way would it resemble my present life. I felt relieved to know I would not have to endure living with a person I feared much longer. I had been trying to put off the inevitable, but the time to take legal action was not far off. In the meantime I had to find a way to change negative into positive in order to survive. I imagined my new home, what it would look like, how it would feel—how wonderful life would be.

Without Bob.

CHAPTER NINETEEN

Michelle was my greatest supporter. She gave me a pep talk about the future and how independent I would be after I completed my college degree.

> *You had hoped to keep her and Eric uninvolved in the Bob mess, said Ms. Freud, but that was no longer possible.*

I assumed the large, gift-wrapped box in the basement was a present for Eric's birthday. I was not surprised Bob had not said one word about it. What surprised me was how little it bothered me.

> *Making progress, smiled Ms. Freud.*

The past two days had been dismal. When the sun finally came out I grabbed my beach bag and hurried off. I made the foolish mistake of returning home before dinner time. Bob waited, poised to pounce the minute I entered the house.

There was:

1. A dent on his car.
2. I bought clothes and he didn't.
3. He no longer had beach club passes because he had given them back to me and therefore expected me to invite him as my guest.
4. He couldn't get Eric or Michelle to commit to an Eric birthday celebration date.

I was certain Bob's anti-anxiety medication was inadequate and he would benefit from additional medication. He confided that on days I crept under his skin, he took two or three pills; he had done that the day before. I wasn't with Bob the day before.

One confused son-of-a-bitch, observed Ms. Freud.

I grabbed my handbag and fled while he was in mid-sentence. I headed for a cozy little restaurant aptly named, "Oasis." Bob must have followed, because he approached my table and acted as if nothing had transpired between us a few moments before.

"Do you mind if I join you?" he inquired. His sardonic smile twisted my stomach into knots. If I allowed Bob to sit down, I would have been as crazy as he was. Not wishing to cause a scene, I stood up and exited the restaurant.

The next morning, I hoped I would see my new acquaintance at the Silver Gull. When I first met Sylvia she was poised near my cafeteria table, waiting for me to look up from my paperback. With my life in turmoil I preferred solitude. I had no desire to engage in conversation with a stranger.

"May I sit?" Sylvia asked, gesturing toward the empty chair.

"As long as you don't talk," I responded.

Before the words were out of my mouth I realized how rude I must have sounded. Sylvia pretended not to notice and promised to be quiet while seating herself across from me. When I finally closed my book and gazed at Sylvia's smiling face, I forgot my no talking rule.

By the time she had finished her lunch, I learned that Sylvia was 10-years my senior and had been divorced many years. She had struggled to put herself through college and worked full-time while raising two children. I sensed that she had experienced her own merry-go-round.

When I got back to the house Bob was in one of his stormy moods. He lectured me about the proper way to re-wind the answering machine tape. I informed him I had recently turned the tape over. Not satisfied, Bob insisted I turn up the volume when the machine is rewinding.

What the hell does one thing have to do with the other, wondered Ms. Freud? This guy had lost any ability to reason.

"It's impossible for me to take you seriously when you think so illogically."

Bob nodded his head in agreement.

"Do you really think you're playing with a full deck?"

"No!"

It was difficult to understand how Bob would acknowledge his disordered mind, but could not see how it was impacting our marriage.

I spent the evening in my room making phone calls. Bob was listening in on the extension, but that was nothing new. He often revealed information he would never have known if he had not eavesdropped on my conversations. I had learned to monitor what I said on the telephone.

He ran up and down the stairs, stopping to ask some inane question each time he passed my room. It was obvious that my phone calls were the source of his anxiety.

The following night Bob had not called home by 11 p.m. It was not unusual for him to disappear to destinations unknown. I had learned not to question him if I didn't want my head ripped off, chewed up and spit out. I went to bed, making sure to secure my bedroom door.

And I finally consulted a lawyer regarding my legal rights.

Mr. Charles' storefront office was close to where I worked and he was often available on the spur of the moment. He charged $25 for an office visit, and if I needed to put recent events in perspective he would dispense advice over the telephone. He never failed to remind me that I was tempting fate by remaining with Bob.

My jigsaw puzzle—the real one in my room—was coming together nicely. Working on the puzzle helped me escape the snake-pit in which I lived.

And the tulip bulbs I planted in the front yard were in full bloom.

Reading about relationships was like locking the barn after the horse was gone, but I figured better late, than never. I learned that the first rule for choosing a partner was to look for someone possessing maturity and emotional stability. There was no room in a relationship for infidelity.

A light bulb moment, said Ms. Freud.

When I made my list of pros and cons before I married Bob, I had forgotten to include those attributes.

CHAPTER TWENTY

As we moved closer to D-Day—For Decision; Death of a marriage; possibly Divorce—life itself moved inexorably onward.

Bob's mother Bea wanted me to arrange Bob's 50th birthday celebration. Because of the marital discord, I tried to convince her how difficult it would be for me to plan a party—even though she offered to pay all expenses.

And Bob did zip last year for your milestone birthday, recalled Ms. Freud.

My plea not to become involved fell on deaf ears; Bea repeated the request.

I told her I would have to think about it, but that whatever I came up with would be expensive. Once again, she reassured me that money was no object.

"With money you get honey," she said, and not once during the entire conversation did she acknowledge that my marriage to her son was at death's door.

Which speaks for itself, offered Ms. Freud.

After Bea's call I was unable to concentrate when I met with Ellen, a student along with me in my American Sign Language (ASL) class—a class chosen to satisfy my bachelor's degree language requirement.

Before Ellen, I was finding it difficult to get through the ASL class. When I chose ASL I was under the misconception that learning hand gestures in lieu of a foreign language would be a piece of cake.

How wrong you were, said Ms. Freud.

Not only was the instructor a tough task-master, but I discovered I had a problem decoding mirror-images. My comprehension was better when standing side-by-side with the person signing than when I faced them.

Ellen was one of the younger students and she had an incredible signing talent. My ASL problems found her offering to tutor me for a nominal fee. She was recently divorced and understood how important it was for me to pass. Whenever I became frustrated we would take a break and talk about her goal to become a psychotherapist for the hearing impaired community.

But after Bea's call I was unable to concentrate when I met with Ellen. Instead of her tutoring me, the entire hour was devoted to therapy—and by the time we arrived in class I felt less angry about my involvement with Bob's celebration.

There was another reason Bob's birthday was such a touchy subject. I resented the times he overlooked my birthday or created turmoil when he did remember. For example, I always wanted to have brunch on the World Yacht while sailing around Manhattan Island. Bob promised to make reservations the next time he was in the city.

My excitement was short-lived. He called from the pier to tell me we would not be going on the World Yacht.

He went on to explain, "I was about to sign the credit card receipt when the gal told me I would have to wear a jacket. I told her I don't wear a jacket for anybody and who did she think she was talking to?"

There was a long pause followed by, "I tore up the receipt and threw it in her face!"

That individual act of rebelliousness was typical. He often objected as well to dressing up when we socialized. On the morning we were going out on the town he would usually ask:

"What are you wearing tonight?"

I rarely made that decision until shortly before I dressed for the evening. After my selection was laid out on the bed, I would summon him for a viewing.

And I hoped that after badgering me all day he would at least choose an appropriate outfit for himself. Instead, he would inevitably pull out a wrinkled pair of khakis and a scuffed pair of shoes. Then he would go to a pile of shirts he had already worn during the week and give them the sniff test before choosing one.

No amount of pleading would alter his decision, said
Ms. Freud. Was he doing this for spite or punishment?

Rather than call attention to the glaring inconsistencies in our attire, I reluctantly dressed-down, choosing a more subdued outfit. In comparison to our friends I often appeared miserably understated.

And Bob looked like a slob, said Ms. Freud.

When I called Michelle and told her about the World Yacht fiasco, she offered no surprise. But her mood picked up when she noted her boss had just received a press release announcing that Cher was going to appear in Atlantic City.

I had always wanted to see Cher in person. Michelle volunteered to call Bob and ask if she should make reservations.

She did—and Bob gave his credit card information and permission to take care of everything. The show tickets were $200 each and because she booked the late show we had to stay overnight. Before she was through, Michelle had charged an all-inclusive weekend package.

Sounds like your little girl was getting even for everything Bob had put her mommy through, said Ms. Freud.

After much agonizing over the promise to Bea to plan Bob's party, I relented and invited eight of our friends to the world famous Peter Luger's for Bob's birthday dinner. The restaurant was known for fabulous steaks and equally fabulous prices.

I had always day-dreamed about riding in a limousine and thought this would be the perfect opportunity to live that dream. I reserved a Lincoln Continental stretch limousine to pick-up Bea and Ernie, Michelle and Eric, and Bob and myself at our house.

I imagined the limousine was there for my celebration. Michelle was annoyed that I didn't charge the limousine to Bea.

Not easy to explain how you were finally doing something for you, sighed Ms. Freud.

When the big evening arrived Bob:

1. Argued with the driver about how to get to the restaurant.
2. Insisted the guests who were already seated when we arrived, stand up.
3. And after they reluctantly complied with his request, he instructed them to sit in a specific order.

Could this be how musical chairs were played in the City of Bedlam, wondered Ms. Freud?

At the end of the evening Bob insisted we come back to the house to see his new deck—the now infamous deck built while he was having his New Orleans breakdown. Four friends begged off—and for my sake I believed the other four agreed to meet us.

We were not expecting company and the only refreshments we had were a half-eaten box of pretzel rods and a few cans of soda. When I suggested we stop to pick up snacks, Bob refused.

The evening was all about him and his deck that stretched before us like the deck of an abandoned ship. Though the hour was late the faithful stood staring at one another, a pretzel rod in one hand and a few inches of plastic cup encased cola in the other—in turn gushing over the deck Bob otherwise hardly set foot upon.

But during the deck unveiling, I focused on my first limousine ride—the smell of new leather and the endless possibilities that lay ahead.

CHAPTER TWENTY ONE

Bob resembled a malfunctioning toy. The packaging was enticing, but once outside the box his operation failed miserably. I grew weary of constant disappointment and frustration alternating with sadness and fear, hoping Bob would change.

Why couldn't you just let go, asked Ms. Freud?

I often took refuge at the beach, carrying my sand chair to a remote area where I would be alone.

With my thoughts. With my tears.

I diffused the despair by writing in a notebook.

> *The sea is there to remind me…to remember times gone by.*
> *Thoughts roll in on the waves and make me cry.*
> *The sea is there to comfort…the sea is there to heal.*
> *The sea is never ending.*
> *I love the sea…it makes me feel.*

By the time I finished writing, I had stopped crying. I was uncertain what had soothed me—putting pen to paper or observing baby sandpipers dancing up and down the shoreline.

The particular day turned out to be exquisite. I decided to stay late and have dinner with friends Scott and Steve. When the conversation took a serious turn, we discussed dragging emotional baggage into relationships. After a short debate about who had the most baggage, I was certain if this were a contest, I would win first prize. I had spent a lifetime trying to lose my emotional baggage or at least store it in my sub-conscious.

The dinner conversation proved to be cathartic. We spoke from the depths of our souls and treated each other with unconditional, positive regard. The evening ended with the realization that I needed to purge myself of the painful emotions I had buried within. Before I went to sleep that night, I prepared a letter I planned to give Bob the next morning.

Dear Bob,

If I leave you a note you get angry. When I talk to you, you ignore me or say, "I don't need this aggravation first thing in the morning" (or before you go to bed, or whenever). There is no right time to approach you. Your mind is so befuddled you don't remember what we discuss and you are constantly asking me, "When did I say that" or "When did you tell me that?"

One thing has become painfully clear. During this period of house separation I have become a non-person. I lost the capable, confident me...the person I used to respect. My every thought, my actions, revolves around you. Not out of respect or love, but out of the desire to avoid confrontation. I can not make the simplest decision without agonizing over how you will react and how I will respond to your reaction.

During my lifetime I have been responsible for a household, an office, other people's children, my child, a husband. I have advised people, directed people, protected people, budgeted money, prepared nutritious meals, and been neat, clean and appropriately attired. I am a good citizen, a good friend, a good mother and a faithful and dutiful wife. I have surmounted obstacles and achieved goals. This wonderful person—me—does not deserve what you have put me through. Recently, this wonderful person who once enjoyed people and life's simple pleasures, felt confident, competent and appreciated, resurfaced. I am back with a vengeance.

There have always been signs of trouble in our relationship dating back to when you flew into a rage after a police officer issued a ticket for double-parking. I dreaded the winters when I was expected to shift into low-gear while you suffered through your winter doldrums. I have tried to be patient, supportive, loving and faithful.

Who paid for our vacations, entertainment, my personal expenses and Michelle's college tuition? I did. I never whined or nagged about what I wanted or what we did not have. I thought I was being a good wife by picking up the slack financially, leaving you free to concentrate on day-to-day expenses and supposedly save for our future. You enjoyed playing, "the king is in the counting room" after cashing your paycheck. How powerful you must have felt kneeling beside the bed counting out your little piles of money and planning your life of deceit.

You claim I make you angry. You were angry long before we met. Therapy helped you deal with the anger you felt toward you mother, but your anger toward me escalated. You were angry when I worked part-time in a real estate office to earn extra money and when I enrolled in college. I did this for us.

Early on I honestly believed I could fix what was wrong with our marriage before it imploded. Now I know I took on an impossible task. Like an engineer struggling to keep the train on schedule I ignored the signals warning of trouble down the line. Instead, I blew through the crossings hoping to arrive at my destination unscathed.

I have observed you juggling the schedule for your anti-anxiety pill as if it were a magic potion expected to solve your problems. I wonder if your mental state deteriorated because of day-to-day stress, or if meeting Eric and his parents put you over the edge. The reason doesn't really matter. I believe the forces that drive you are far greater than you perceive. You have rejected additional medication in conjunction with therapy, but the time has come for you to reconsider your decision.

I can no longer allow you to abuse me verbally, emotionally or physically. To continue living under the same roof serves no purpose. Unless you or Dr. Adler has something to say about continuing this relationship the only solution is to enter into a formal separation agreement.

Lee

After securing my bedroom door I clutched Teddy tightly. The plush bear was a gift from my brother. When locked in my room at night, Teddy's presence comforted me. He was my guardian, my confidant, my friend. I fell into a restless sleep.

Before we left on vacation Bob packed every article of clothing he owned. I did exactly the same thing hoping he would see how irrational his actions were. When it came time to return home, Bob was nowhere to be found. When I packed for both of us, I discovered duplicate items of clothing and items he had no use for. I was not surprised. He often made senseless purchases and became defensive if I questioned him about them.

In the morning I handed Bob the letter written the night before. I suggested he read it before our next counseling session. He accepted it without saying a word, picked up his attaché case and continued out the front door.

When Bob returned home that evening he did not mention the letter. Instead he told me a cousin had died and he planned to attend the funeral. He asked if I would accompany him; I declined.

That night I dreamed about my mother.

An older woman carrying a beach chair befriended me. She had emerged from a maroon Nash Rambler similar to the car my grandfather drove in Florida, forty years earlier. The woman offered me a ride to my hotel. I suspected we were going in opposite directions, not unlike when my mother was alive and we could not agree on anything. The woman assured me my destination was not a problem. I accepted her offer.

The last time I looked in the green metal box in our bedroom closet, I discovered two small, red envelopes that had not been there previously. Each contained a key to a safety deposit box. When I slipped them into my pocket I was already planning which bank I would visit first and what to say when I got there.

I would begin with banks closest to home and work my way toward Bea's neighborhood and then on to the area where Bob worked. I didn't have far to go before finding the right bank. I approached the attendant seated at the desk in front of the vault and handed her the envelopes containing the keys.

"I hope you can help me. I've been trying to identify these keys."

"Yes, these are our envelopes. Did you find these keys?"

It only took a moment to formulate a little white lie about my father passing away.

"My dad just…" Before I could finish the attendant interrupted.

"You poor thing, you have my deepest sympathy. Just give me both your names and I'll check the log-in register."

I couldn't continue the charade.

"I have to apologize. I'm embarrassed to admit it, but I am really here to check up on my husband."

"You aren't the first and you won't be the last," the attendant chuckled, shaking her head.

She remembered Bob because he had difficulty understanding who would have access to the safety deposit boxes. In the end, he named me as Deputy—which meant I could have access at anytime—and something the attendant thought Bob was unclear about when he left the bank.

"Would you like to go into the vault?"

"Yes please. Yes, I would," I said, handing the attendant my photo ID and signing the entry log.

With two metal boxes cradled in my arms the attendant ushered me into a private room. At first I sat transfixed, unable to process the events of the last few minutes. I had no idea what to expect when I lifted the first latch and peered inside.

The first box was empty?

I was certain Bob needed a place to hide evidence of some wrongdoing. The second box contained the checkbook linked to the home equity loan.

After searching the check register, I discovered Bob had not paid for Michelle and Eric's new kitchen cabinets out of our savings account. When he made the magnanimous gesture to pay for cabinets, he never told me the money was coming from the home equity account.

What was even more upsetting were the entries for checks payable to Bob's brother.

I removed the checkbook and rang for the attendant. After a little banking of my own, I left feeling victorious.

CHAPTER TWENTY TWO

D-Day had finally arrived.

I planned to meet Bob in Dr. Adler's office to discuss the Decision: Death of a marriage and perhaps Divorce.

Bob was already dressed and sitting rigidly at the kitchen table. He suggested we go out for breakfast.

I refused to join him.

We met at Dr. Adler's office at the appointed time where we thumbed through outdated magazines with feigned interest. When Dr. Adler opened the door he motioned for Bob to enter and motioned for me to remain seated.

I was unaware Bob had called ahead and requested they speak in private before our scheduled session. I had planned to discuss my visit to the bank when we were with Dr. Adler, but before I had a chance Bob tore into me.

"I just came from the bank. Why in hell did you cancel the home equity line of credit?" Bob shook his fist menacingly. "There's money missing from our joint account. Where is it?"

The menacing fist continued.

Attempting to calm him, Dr. Adler assured Bob there was a logical explanation if he would allow me to respond.

I explained that Mr. Charles advised me to satisfy the outstanding loan with funds from our joint account and cancel the home equity loan. He believed a large credit line was too tempting during this time of marital discord.

Dr. Adler nodded, satisfied with my explanation.

As long as we were discussing bank activity I brought up transferring money—and money disappearing without a trace.

You suspected Bob was investing money with his brother, Ms. Freud said, or he was using Allan as a cover for a secret bank account.

Bob bellowed when I mentioned that numerous checks from the home equity account had been made payable to Allan. "He's my brother and I can give him as much money as I damn please," he yelled.

Eventually, we moved from money to "no ROI." Each winter when Bob withdrew emotionally and physically he often used "no return on investment" as an excuse for his sexual inactivity. Asked to elaborate, he replied, "I'm not ready to discuss that yet."

When I asked Bob why he carried condoms after I had my tubes tied, Dr. Adler and I were astounded by his reply. "I carry them in case I get lucky," he reasoned—and then accused me of not being sensitive to his needs.

If that were true, Ms. Freud reasoned, you would not have tried so hard to keep the marriage intact.

Our emotions had been laid bare. An icy stillness fell over the room until Dr. Adler turned to face Bob.

"We have heard how your self-serving actions impact your relationship with Lee. This is a good time for you to express any thoughts you may have regarding what we discussed today." Bob placed two fingers across his lips, the signal that spoke volumes.

After a short pause, Dr. Adler continued. "I think the next step would be for the two of you to work on a separation agreement.

We can review it during our next session and I can mediate any disagreements."

On the way out Bob muttered something about discussing his concerns over coffee. Reluctance gave way to weariness and a cup of coffee sounded like a good idea. After placing our order Bob lowered his voice. "My greatest concern is telling Michele and Eric we are separating. Is there a possibility of getting back together after a year or so?"

"For that to occur, you would have to move in with Dr. Adler and undergo therapy 24/7."

We burst out laughing. When the laughter subsided, I assured Bob nothing was impossible. There was no further discussion about a separation agreement or the letter I had given him earlier.

The next morning Bob was outside at the crack of dawn. It sounded like I was being awakened by a leaf blower, and when I looked through the window I noticed the tulips I had planted, watered and nurtured had disappeared from the front yard.

I ran downstairs hoping Bob had placed them in a vase. I was cranky from having my sleep disturbed and discovering my beautiful tulips missing. I waited for Bob to come inside before confronting him.

"What the hell happened to my tulips?" I asked angrily.

"I weeded the garden. Everything was dead anyway."

Bob's judgment was impaired along with his memory. I had observed him putting out the garbage cans on the wrong days or forgetting to put them out at all. His confusion was a minor concern compared to his actions.

He was becoming more dangerous and out of control with each passing day. I would often hear him cursing, "That bitch!" through the bathroom door. Whenever Bob took a shower he disconnected the telephone line forcing me to go outside to a pay phone. What made it worse was when I had to explain to Michelle why our phone was out of order.

One morning, I could not find my car keys. I usually left them in the ceramic duck in the kitchen, next to my handbag. I had no choice but to ask Bob if he knew where they were.

"You don't know how cunning I can be; you have no idea what I could do to your car," he said, sneering.

I felt my adrenaline surge. Could he have cut the brake line or planted an explosive in my car?

This bullshit is making you late, chided Ms. Freud.

"Cut the crap and give me my damn keys!" I demanded.

Bob appeared startled and immediately retrieved the keys.

I feared for my life more with each passing day. Bob would erupt without warning, bulging veins pulsating on either sides of his neck while he shook fists in my face. I once asked if he were going to hit me.

"I've wanted to for a long time," was his reply. I secretly wished he would assault me. I would be forced to take out an Order of Protection. Instead, I was stuck.

Co-dependency's a bitch, mused Ms. Freud.

CHAPTER TWENTY THREE

Once a month, a group of co-workers met at a local pub to complain about the workload and share a few laughs. Close friendships were forged and even an occasional flirtation. I found myself attracted to Jim.

I felt protected when I was in his presence. He and my dad shared similar characteristics; they were bald, mustached and soft-spoken.

We discussed a variety of topics, from the importance for married men to carry life insurance to his belief that "only stupid people lease cars."

We also debated the pros and cons of legalized prostitution. Jim enlightened me to the number of males dressed as females who solicited businessmen outside the entrance to the Holland Tunnel. Married men often stopped to get their "knobs polished," on the way to suburbia, according to Jim.

What concerned me was learning that many street prostitutes were HIV infected. I had all I could do to keep from blurting out my deepest darkest secret—not knowing if Bob was fish or fowl or a bit of both.

More to the point, worrying about the festering blister on his pubis that he covered with a Band-aid, said Ms. Freud.

When I asked, he insisted there was nothing to worry about.

I thought about the complementary newspapers Bob brought home from business trips—the ones available in public places. Many would often be turned to the section advertising male on male liaisons. When I mustered the courage to ask about his interest in the ads and if he is homosexual, he replied, "You're being ridiculous," before he stormed out of the room.

I've never been a homophobe. There were gay relatives on both sides of the family, but in my mind that increased the possibility Bob was homosexual. We were acquainted with previously closeted males who were unsuccessful in attempts to exist in a traditional marriage. Eventually most moved on to homosexual relationships.

Was Bob like that, wondered Ms. Freud?

The possibility that Bob could be bi-sexual concerned me even more. In fact, the thought frightened and repulsed me, but I wasn't sure why. I remembered when I opened Bob's car trunk and a hot-pink, feather floated skyward. It reminded me of a cheap feather boa, used by exotic dancers and female impersonators.

I slammed the trunk shut the same way I shut my mind at the end of my conversation with Jim. It was too much information to sort out on my own.

During my next session with Dr. Adler I mentioned Bob's promiscuity and the possibility of contracting HIV. I was surprised at his suggestion that Bob and I undergo testing. I was certain convincing Bob would be difficult, if not impossible.

I made sure I had all the procedural information before I broached the subject. When I explained that Dr. Adler was in favor of our being tested, Bob seemed surprisingly amenable to the idea. I didn't think he fully comprehended the seriousness of that which we were about to embark on.

Since the entire process was confidential we had to call the Department of Health separately to secure individual identification numbers. There would be a waiting period of at least a week before we would learn the outcome. We decided to be tested in Manhattan.

Before being called to the lab we were each assigned a counselor. I was asked if I suspected I had been exposed to HIV and what I would do if the test results came back positive. I answered the questions thoughtfully and honestly.

And how did Bob answer, wondered Ms. Freud?

I could hear him laughing in the next office the entire time spent with his counselor. I had already made up my mind, regardless of the outcome I would not, could not, remain married to Bob.

After the ordeal was over Bob offered to drop me off in midtown Manhattan on the way to a business appointment. Of course, the thought did cross my mind that he may be off to see a hooker.

We spent the next week going about the day-to-day business of living while trying to have as little to do with each other as possible. Neither of us spoke during the return trip to Manhattan. I felt as if I were going to an execution when we approached to the dismal, grey New York State Board of Health building. Bob appeared unconcerned and even stopped for a newspaper to check the Manhattan movie schedule. I did not trust Bob to be truthful about his test results. I was surprised when he agreed to hear our reports read in each other's presence. Our counselors had to obtain permission from a superior before complying with this request.

When we were called in to the office where both counselors waited I was a nervous wreck. I was relieved to learn we both tested negative. Bob shook hands with the counselors and brazenly commented:

"I don't know what she was worried about; I told her I was careful." I felt mortified as he continued his smug comments. "You made such a fuss over nothing."

We rode the elevator to the street without speaking. By the time we exited the building I felt physically ill and I could not bear to be in Bob's presence another moment.

I left him standing at the curb, fuming. We had the rest of the day to spend in the city and I deserted him. I continued to walk until I could no longer hear him sputtering.

The autumn chill stung my nose, cheeks and fingertips. But the discomfort was minor compared to the pain tearing at my heart.

CHAPTER TWENTY FOUR

I spoke to Michelle about spending Saturday together. She begged off, but promised to let me know if plans changed. When she had not called by mid-day I headed toward the local mall.

Traffic was heavy and the drive took longer than I anticipated. As I walked through the parking lot, I heard a voice in the distance screaming "Ma! Ma!"

I turned around and recognized Michelle running toward me, tears streaming. She threw herself into my arms, sobs muffling words. For a moment, I imagined somebody had died.

I grabbed her shoulders and gently pushed her away. I wanted to see her face.

"What's wrong? What happened?"

She hesitated, trying to compose herself. "I'm so glad I found you."

"Did something happen to Eric or Bob?"

"No, but Bob is really pissed."

"That's nothing new. What is it this time?"

"I tried to catch you before you left the house. I wanted to tell you I could meet you after all. I didn't want to talk to Bob, but he answered the phone and one word led to another..."

"Michelle! Don't keep me in suspense. What happened?"

"I must have said something he didn't like and he said, "Fuck you, Michelle!"

"And then what happened?"

"I knew it was wrong ma, but I couldn't help myself."

"You're killing me here; finish the story!"

"I said, 'Fuck you, Bob!' And after I said it I knew I had to find you or you wouldn't know what to expect when you arrived home."

What could I possibly say, my child was hurting and she was worried about me. She wanted to spare me the pain. I pulled her toward me and kissed her forehead.

"Knowing you as I do, you must have wanted to say that for a long time and held back until now."

"You're not mad, Ma?"

"No! I'm not mad. I'm glad you found me."

We walked into the mall arm-in-arm.

When I returned home neither Bob nor I mentioned the incident.

Later, a newspaper advertisement caught my eye with the question: "Are you stuck in a relationship and don't know what to do about it?"

The ad implied that the problem could be resolved through short-term behavioral therapy. I dialed the number and scheduled an appointment for the following week. I had no idea what to expect when I pushed the button to gain entry into the residential building.

Emma Levy, LSW greeted me as I stepped into a sparsely furnished apartment devoid of books, pictures, or framed credentials.

What have you gotten yourself into now, wondered Ms. Freud?

Our conversation evolved into Emma not understanding why I planned to move out of my house instead of Bob leaving. Asking him to vacate the premises was not an option. When I once suggested he leave, he roared so loud, "This is my house and I'm not going anywhere!"

You thought the windows would shatter, said Ms. Freud.

Each session with Emma was a carbon copy of the previous one. She asked what I had done for myself the previous week and if I had read a self-help book from her recommended reading list. No matter how I responded, Emma sounded disappointed. I could never do enough to please her. She didn't understand how difficult it was to fit anything else into my hectic schedule. I was driving an hour each way to work, attending college two nights each week in the dead of winter and sleeping in my barricaded bedroom.

I was having trouble eating and I continued to lose weight. I was already gravely stressed and she was beginning to piss me off. I fantasized about telling her off and not coming back.

At one session Emma offered that Bob likely met the criteria for borderline personality disorder. According to the *Diagnostic and Statistical Manual of the American Psychiatric Association (DSM-IV)* people with borderline personality disorder exhibit a pervasive pattern of instability in interpersonal relationships, self-image, and affects, and marked impulsivity beginning in early adulthood.

In an effort to understand more about what made Bob tick, I finally found time to read one of the books Emma recommended. After I finished reading *I Hate You. Don't Leave Me—Understanding the Borderline Personality*, I regretted not having read it sooner. It would have helped me understand the futility in trying to make sense of Bob's behavior.

After a month of meeting with Emma, and in what seemed like a senseless waste of time and money, my car was stolen. I had the additional burden of nearly freezing to death atop mounds of ice and snow waiting for a bus to work. Attending evening classes meant I had to arrange rides with classmates.

One Saturday, Michelle treated me to lunch. I told her there was no way I would be able to keep my next appointment with Emma. I dreaded having to cancel. I was certain she would reprimand me and I was in no mood to deal with her. I began to cry. That wasn't at all like me. I was usually strong as a rock, but this rock was beginning to crumble.

You felt defeated, said Ms. Freud.

Michelle volunteered to make the phone call and offered to tell Emma I was never coming back. I promised Michelle I would handle it, and when I finally did call, Emma was unsympathetic and would not accept my excuse. After arguing back and forth she finally agreed to cancel one session. She made it clear she expected to meet with me the following week.

At the same time, I never thought I would see my car again until the police called with the news that it had been abandoned. The grill and radio were missing, but I didn't care what condition my car was in as long as it was returned.

When I met with Emma, I unleashed emotions I had bottled up for a long while.

"You call yourself a therapist? Is that what we have been doing here, therapy? You have no compassion, no empathy; you don't have a clue what I have been going through!" I shouted. "I'm living in a crazy house, my car was stolen and you expect me to read stupid books and answer your annoying questions!"

When there was nothing left to say a smile crept across Emma's face. I was surprised that she was not angry.

Instead of reprimanding me she sounded delighted. "We've done good work here; you've finally gotten in touch with your anger. Now you can move on, you're ready to take the next step—to do whatever is necessary to experience the life you deserve. You don't need me anymore."

At that moment I understood, the badgering, the reprimands—all part of a process. Apologizing for my outburst, I thanked Emma; I would no longer stuff my anger.

I felt hungry for the first time in months.

Michelle and I spent the next weekend apartment hunting. Every apartment we looked at was worse than the one before. Each was reminiscent of the hellholes I had lived in when I was single. I could never go back. Never. Ever.

My ever resourceful daughter suggested instead of looking for a one-bedroom apartment I should look for a studio apartment in a better neighborhood. We agreed to try again the following week.

I felt stronger, more focused. I had a beautiful daughter, friends, and a good job. I felt in control, empowered. Bob had made me give up so much. He had torn me apart. There had been times when I could not talk to Michelle, hug or kiss her, spend time with her. She should not have to feel afraid to phone me or visit my house. Those days would soon be over.

And then the clock on the nightstand glared at me. It was barely 3 a.m.

Pounding on my bedroom door? Was there a fire? Was Bob in distress?

"What's the matter? What's wrong?" I called out, frantically.

My words were met with silence. I unwound the television cord from around my doorknob and pushed the night table and television set away from the door. I fully expected to find a hallway filled with smoke or Bob clutching his chest in the throes of a heart attack.

Instead, I found him standing in front of my door with his robe untied and his genitals exposed. His maniacal grin was reminiscent of Jack Nicholson in *The Shining*.

My heart pounded as I bombarded Bob with questions.

"What's wrong with you? Why didn't you answer me? Didn't you hear me?"

"Scared you, didn't I?" Bob chortled, like a deviant child playing a prank.

If the scene were not so bizarre it would have been comical.

"If you ever do a stupid thing like that again," I shouted while wagging my finger in his face, "I promise to call Dr. Adler and your mother! Do you understand me?"

Bob's demeanor took a 360 degree turn. After he was chastised by the authority figure, the obedient child snapped to attention and retreated to his bedroom.

The next morning I rushed off hoping I would meet up with my friend Sandy before students arrived. I desperately needed to talk to her about the previous night. My heart pounded when I spotted her standing near the time clock. She took one look at my face and knew I needed to talk. I calmed down only after we agreed to meet for lunch. How lucky I was to have a friend who understood exactly what I was going through.

Turns out Bob had a lot in common with Sandy's brother, said Ms. Freud.

"You know you have to get out of there don't you?" Sandy queried.

I nodded.

"I know financially you're not prepared to leave." Sandy reached inside her purse and after a brief search handed me a business card. "This is the telephone number for the 24-hour Mobile Crisis Intervention Unit. Always have it handy. You never know when you'll need it." Sandy's close friends knew she was dealing with her own family drama. She must have used the card on more than one occasion. I could not believe my life had come to this.

Taking the card from Sandy, I suddenly realized: "Wasn't Son of Sam held in this same psychiatric facility?"

"Yeah—and they loaded him up with Thorazine and Librium, like they should do to Bob."

"Thorazine, the stuff that produces a chemical lobotomy. I can't believe they're still using that crap!"

I knew I could never dial the number on the card. It would be impossible for me to be the one responsible for locking Bob away.

At the same time a multitude of mentally ill people accepted a need for daily medication and existed outside such institutions.

You just happen to have a guy that needs meds big time and refuses to take them, said Ms. Freud.

CHAPTER TWENTY FIVE

The stress of dealing with Bob was becoming insufferable. I began experiencing chest pains. I considered making an appointment with a cardiologist, but I decided to visit Bea first.

She welcomed me warmly and then scrutinized me at arms length. "What is it—what's wrong?"

I felt like my insides were on fire. My words caught us both by surprise.

"My life has become unbearable I can't take it anymore. I tried so hard to be there for Bob, but he blames me for everything. I can't deal with his mood swings and his threats. He's completely out of control—I'm afraid of what he is capable of doing."

"He pays the bills, doesn't he?" Bea asked.

She can't be that naïve, said Ms. Freud.

I said: "What does that have to do with anything?"

Bea took my hand in hers and squeezed it tightly. "I'm so sorry this is happening to you, but now you know what I went through all these years."

Bea bowed her head and silently wept. This was the first time she validated my struggle to help Bob and keep our marriage intact. We were two caring women who fought the good fight until we were all used up. My chest pains subsided after I unloaded my burden.

Michelle had spoken to a landlord who had a studio apartment in an upscale neighborhood. I called and arranged to see the apartment that evening.

The entrance was located in the rear of a three-family house. After I walked through a lovely garden, I faced the rear of a large apartment building where I imagined a million eyes would watch my every move.

My concerns vanished when I realized it wasn't necessarily a bad thing. I hoped the neighbors would be my guardian angels and keep me safe from harm. I would have to overlook the tiny bathroom, outdated linoleum and old refrigerator, but I was certain I would thrive in this isolated sanctuary.

I planned to move sooner than anticipated. That meant my income would be inadequate until after graduation. The landlord wanted more rent than I could afford. When he agreed to reduce the amount for one year I was certain Michelle made a convincing sales pitch on my behalf. I could imagine her telling the landlord John, "You'll never regret having my mother for a tenant and by the way, if she doesn't get out of her house my step-father will kill her."

I felt relieved until reality set in. I would have to face Bob with the news that I was leaving and I had to work out the logistics of moving some of my possessions to the new apartment.

I would not take everything. I believed the move was only temporary. I was certain our separation would prompt Bob to do whatever necessary to rectify the situation. I imagined him calling one day to tell me how much he loved me and missed me and how sorry he was for the way he behaved. He would be miraculously cured, and beg me to come home.

I was also not looking forward to leaving behind all that was familiar. I felt like a frightened child during a family outing, now lost in the woods with darkness descending.

I delayed telling Bob my moving plans. I was petrified when I imagined how he would react. The longer I waited the more anxious I became. After a night of tossing and turning, sitting up and lying down, and praying for dawn to arrive, I found the courage to tell Bob I rented an apartment and I was moving out.

"OK," he said.

Just "OK?"

And in that moment everything *was* OK. It didn't matter that Bob showed not one iota of emotion, or remorse—or even anger.

Nothing.

I felt as if I were floating in a pool of warm water—weightless, peaceful and emancipated.

CHAPTER TWENTY SIX

In the weeks that followed—and with Dr. Adler's help—we hammered out an informal separation agreement

1. I was free to take up residence elsewhere and I had 30 days in which to vacate the jointly owned premises.

2. No loans could be made against the house.

3. No alterations could be made to structure, furnishings or décor.

4. Bob would remain in the house and continue to maintain and insure the premises.

5. I agreed to keep Bob covered under my health insurance and he agreed to continue paying for my car insurance.

6. In the event the one year separation resulted in divorce, Bob would buy me out—after the balance of the mortgage was satisfied.

7. We waved the right to each others pensions.

8. Neither of us would request alimony.

I packed for four days, but was doubtful I would be ready to move on time. A friend had advised me to put clothes in large trash bags. Michelle, Eric and a friend Mark were due to arrive at 10 a.m., and that meant we would have three cars.

Earlier that morning, I had declined Bob's offer to go out for breakfast. He had no concept of my priorities or that I was mentally and physically exhausted with even being in his presence.

When the Three Musketeers arrived at the appointed time, Bob kissed Michelle on the cheek and shook hands with Eric and Mark. He helped carry cartons out to my car while I finished packing. After loading the three cars, there were still items remaining which we planned to pick up later in the day.

A light drizzle was falling while we tied the mattress from Michelle's old room to the roof of my car. When we pulled away from the curb, I glanced back at the cozy house that had been my home. Bob stood on the porch, waiving hesitantly. I felt as if my heart would break.

We worked quickly to unload the cars and carry everything inside. Mark suggested a pizza celebration and insisted on treating us. We busied ourselves unpacking cartons while Mark went out to pick up pizza and soda. It was not long before he returned with lunch, a newspaper, container of imported apricots and a gigantic package of paper plates.

After lunch Mark volunteered to set-up my new answering machine. He insisted we record a masculine voice since I was a woman living alone. Eric suggested we bark like dogs to make the message sound more menacing. When we pressed the record button Mark snarled, "There's nobody here to answer your call… leave a message at the beep," while Michelle, Eric and I barked and howled. By the time the message was recorded, we were laughing hysterically.

When we arrived back to pick up the remainder, Bob suggested we go out for lunch.

Doesn't he realize how absurd that invitation is under the circumstances, asked Ms. Freud?

He scowled upon learning we had already eaten, but quickly changed the subject and accused me of taking a framed picture of Michelle, which he claimed she had given him as a gift. Michelle told Bob he was mistaken. The gift was for both of us and since she was my daughter the picture rightfully belonged to me. Bob dropped the argument.

I took the opportunity to mention that I could not find Eric and Michelle's wedding albums. One contained the photographer's pictures and the other was compiled of Mark's snapshots.

Bob gave the excuse that he could not locate them at that moment. I remembered the albums disappeared around the time he changed the lock on the garage and the key was never made available to me. I surmised the albums were locked in his private storage area.

Along with God only knows what else, said Ms. Freud.

This time when we drove away I did not look back. The rain stopped and the sun emerged from behind a cloud.

It was an omen.

Before leaving that night, Michelle made up my bed. Teddy was on the pillow and tucked in up to his chin with his front paws on top of the quilt. I was reminded of the times I tucked her in and the years we had lost. This loving gesture from daughter to mother will remain etched in my heart forever.

PART FOUR

THE RIDE'S NOT OVER

CHAPTER TWENTY SEVEN

My dad called to find out how the move went. I was happy to report the worst was over. He had tried to contact me once before, but when he heard a man's voice on the answering machine he hung up. After my brother related a similar experience, I recorded a new message in my own voice and omitted the chorus of yapping junk-yard dogs.

I had in fact been afraid of dogs since I was a child. My mother would pull me into a doorway whenever a dog approached. And I felt apprehensive at my new apartment when I noticed the large grey and white Akita with steel blue eyes in the adjoining backyard. Eventually I overcame the fear and considered Blue my personal watchdog.

A young man lived in the apartment above mine. Late at night, the sound of his footsteps comforted me. When we met Mel seemed anxious to chat. His rental agreement stipulated that he shoveled the walkways after a snowfall and put the garbage cans at the curb twice a week. He asked if I would help out by wheeling the cans back to the storage bin after they were emptied. And so began a relationship where we looked out for one another.

On snowy mornings I would hear Mel's melodious voice, "Lee, are you in there?" followed by the sound of his shovel scraping concrete as he cleared a path to my door. When the snowfall occurred on a weekend I would help Mel shovel the snow and afterwards we would trudge off in search of a hot breakfast at the neighborhood coffee shop.

An old friend I had known as a teenager called to invite me for a drink. He wanted to counsel me on my re-entry into the single's world. Dr. Steven Feinstein was already in a committed relationship, but wanted to see me for "old times" sake.

I remembered Steven as a bashful 17-year-old with long, lanky legs and sweaty palms. Our initial outing had been a movie, followed by a visit to an ice cream parlor and a shared milkshake. He walked me home later and after an awkward display of affection, we opted to remain just friends.

I anticipated that this date as true adults would be different when he suggested an intimate lounge for the reunion. We sipped cocktails and watched flickering candlelight cast abstract shadows.

Steven sounded genuinely sorry to learn my life was in turmoil. He reminded me how lucky I was to have a daughter and that he regretted not having children of his own. He insisted I needed to loosen up and dress more provocatively as he reached across the table to unbutton the top two buttons on my severely tailored blouse.

By the end of the evening I realized he hadn't changed much except for acquiring the title, Doctor, which as it turned out was doctor of philosophy, not doctor of medicine.

Occasionally I would experience a vivid dream involving Bob where our love-hate relationship played out. The content was usually sexual, and alternating with acts of aggression. My contact with him became less frequent. Every so often he would call to ask about Michelle and Eric or give me an update on his family—but his words would be punctuated by long pauses as if waiting for something.

Does he want to get together, Ms. Freud mused, or are you projecting your own feelings of isolation?

After Bob called to tell me his step-father was scheduled for open-heart surgery Bea called to find out how I was managing. She believed all that mattered was that everything turned out all right in the end. She did not know if Bob was continuing his therapy because she was afraid to ask personal questions.

I also sensed that she had an ulterior motive for calling—and that turned out to be her husband Ernie's need for blood donations before surgery. The hospital said the donor's blood did not have to match the patient's as long as the blood supply was replenished. Most of Bea's elderly friends had medical problems that rendered them ineligible; Bob was also ineligible to donate.

Bob had been rejected—and I remembered he had been turned down earlier for a life insurance policy as well.

And was the reason he wasn't now permitted to donate blood the same reason he was also turned down for life insurance, queried Ms. Freud?

I didn't think for one moment that I would be rejected, but the idea of donating blood made me queasy. Still, Ernie was such a dear, sweet man and reminded me of my dad; I could not refuse.

Bea would not stop thanking me after I agreed to be a donor. We shared a hearty laugh after I asked her if she thought Ernie would end up with my curly hair if he received my blood. She ended the conversation by telling me she loved me.

CHAPTER TWENTY EIGHT

The Bob related life insurance question I had considered during Ernie's need for blood donors began much earlier.

Before every vacation Bob and I had the same discussion about insurance. It always escalated into an argument, but I remained concerned that if he died I would not be able to afford the mortgage.

Bob always offered the same reason for not taking out a life insurance policy. "I don't want to bet against myself."

He used the same excuse when I brought up mortgage or disability insurance. Bob did not have a will and I was hoping to avoid a legal battle with his family. But when he coerced me into applying for the home equity loan I insisted he stop the BS and take out a life insurance policy.

After examination by a doctor, he was rejected by the insurer.

I was not looking forward to visiting Ernie in the ICU. I knew if I saw him hooked up to machines and tubes it would remind me of my own father's declining health.

When I arrived, Ernie's son, daughter-in-law, Bea and Bob were in the waiting room. Bob wanted to know if I had driven. I had in fact come by train and Michelle would be driving me home when she finished work.

Bob insisted I accompany him to the hospital cafeteria to help carry coffee back to the group. In the elevator, he mentioned missing his last two therapy sessions. I thought it best not to comment.

He second-guessed my every move as we filled the coffee containers. Before I reached for the sugar, the milk or the lid he was already thrusting those toward me with one hand while rhythmically slapping his thigh with the other hand. I recognized the dance of anxiety.

He's self-medicating again and deciding when or if to take his Xanax, said Ms. Freud.

When we returned to the waiting room I located a seat far away from everyone. Bob followed me and suggested he accompany me when I leave the hospital and Michelle would then drop us off at my place.

He frequently mentioned coming to my apartment. It was only after I asked how his mother would get home that he remembered his car was parked in the hospital's garage.

Bob or Bea continued to update me on Ernie's progress. During one of these conversations she revealed news about Bob's brother and sister-in-law.

"Jackie and Allan are getting divorced!"

"What did you say?" not certain I had heard correctly.

"I know. It's hard to believe. They've had their little problems, but I never expected this."

I recalled Jackie's "if looks could kill stare" many times in the past. With everything I was dealing with I had little emotion to spare. "I'm sorry to hear the news," was all I offered.

After Bea's call Bob never mentioned his brother's divorce. He probably filed the information in his mind's "family secrets" drawer.

Our separation, however, didn't stop the dreams. I dreamed Bob was at my place for dinner.

We covered ourselves with a large cloth to keep the overwhelming physical attraction from interfering with our evening. The scene changed to a coffee shop in an upscale hotel where we were joined by two male friends. One of them was an old boyfriend, I was still attracted to. Bob told me he was jealous of my apartment, angry about his real estate taxes and vexed about having to assume so many responsibilities. I asked what that had to do with me. Then, I turned my attention to my old boyfriend who was sorry to hear Bob and I separated. He assured me Bob and another man would be back to see me later that night. I did not appreciate the sexual inference.

This was the first holiday season alone in my new apartment and I was feeling melancholy. To make matters worse, the ejector pump that operated the toilet acted up. Occasionally the rod would stick and the toilet overflowed. The service company had already adjusted the pump twice.

I found myself wondering what Bob was doing until I remembered my inevitable disappointment whenever we spent time together. There was nothing like a walk down memory lane and a malfunctioning ejector pump to change melancholia into anger, and anger into action.

I bundled up and went shopping for Christmas decorations.

There were a few items Bob thought I would want from the house. I suspected he was also looking for an excuse to get together when he suggested we attend the dance where we first met.

And he has no clue how awkward and painful that would be for you, Ms. Freud asked?

144

When he rejected my suggestion to see a movie we decided to meet at a restaurant. During dinner I was reminded of his unrealistic expectations when he expressed a desire to celebrate New Year's Eve with Michelle and Eric.

At the end of the evening I followed him the short distance back to our house to pick up the items he had set aside for me. After he handed me a shopping bag containing nothing of importance, I realized he only used this as an excuse to lure me. When I turned to leave Bob muttered something about spending the night.

Come in to my parlor said the spider to the fly, smiled Ms. Freud.

I quickly left.

CHAPTER TWENTY NINE

I began to dream more frequently.

Bob and I were in a parked car, discussing our current situation. He was back on medication, but as the conversation escalated the look in his eyes grew wilder. When he stood on the front seat making threatening gestures it was as if Lucifer himself were standing before me. There were two unfamiliar sets of keys behind the front seat. One set was larger than the other. Bob did not know if either set belonged to him. Bob followed me when I exited the car.

Landlord John had a new ejector pump installed. While I waited for the plumber, UPS delivered a huge carton from my brother.

Not knowing what to expect, I opened it carefully. Inside was a Tower of Treats consisting of six boxes stacked smallest to largest, tied with a big red ribbon. It seemed a shame to disturb the beautiful arrangement. When I was no longer able to resist, I peaked inside each box.

My senses were treated to the most tantalizing delicacies. I closed my eyes and imagined I was a Queen relishing my kingdom's riches—the treasure that lay before me, gifts from adoring subjects.

Then you otherwise finally began to open your eyes, said Ms. Freud.

That evening I joined my friend Evelyn for dinner, followed by a drive through the neighborhood to view the many Christmas decorations. The evening concluded with us agreeing that all men were immature alley cats without a conscience.

The following week was a frenzy of holiday activities both with friends and at work. It was a time of mixed emotions. The weather was bitterly cold and my stomach was on the fritz. One day I was so tired, I had to take two naps. My VCR also broke and a slight water stain appeared on the bathroom ceiling. I dreaded having to confront Mel about the leak and decided to put it off until after the holidays.

Even though concerned how Bob and I would feel attending the same party so soon after we split-up, Marilyn and Paul extended the annual holiday invitation. This holiday celebration was unique, and I admired how the party seamlessly combined faiths and families.

The Christmas Eve feast reflected the traditions of both families. Before the dining room filled to capacity guests were advised to use the bathroom. Paul assured everyone it would be impossible to get up once everyone was seated—unless the house caught on fire.

After several courses, guests invited for the early seating were ushered into the living room where holiday decorations could be admired and stomachs gain a rest. The second seating consisted of guests who knew the meal would be reheated food, but were happy to be a part of the ritual.

By 10 p.m. the crowd thinned—many off to fulfill other holiday obligations. The remaining guests—as well as late arrivals invited for dessert or a drink—would file into the dining room and join guests already seated.

I felt privileged to receive an invitation to the first seating and I had no intention of missing this special event. Whatever Bob chose to do was of no concern to me.

But I was surprised when Bob called the day before the party. He assumed parking spaces would be scarce on Christmas Eve and suggested we attend together. I made an excuse about not being sure what time I would be ready.

"You always have to make everything more difficult," Bob fumed before hanging up.

We arrived within minutes of each other. Marilyn deliberately seated us on opposite sides of the dining room table. The only time Bob and I interacted was when I asked him to pass a platter of food. To the uninformed observer we were just another married couple enjoying the festivities.

CHAPTER THIRTY

I spent Christmas day with Eric and Michelle. We enjoyed a wonderful dinner and exchanged gifts. In addition to a robe, slippers and my favorite perfume, I was surprised with a new VCR.

The day after Christmas the weather was mild enough to take a long walk through my new neighborhood. The impressive mini-mansions, adorned with Roman columns, were surrounded by neatly manicured lawns. Most of the houses were built on waterfront property with pleasure boats moored behind each home.

I imagined the happy, intact families living in these homes and I became overcome with emotion. My miserable existence unreeled like a grainy silent film. Bob destroyed every happy moment in my life. I could not experience the joy of my daughter's bridal shower or wedding for fear he would flip out. I suppressed my own thoughts and desires and walked on eggshells for so long. I barely existed in a one-room apartment and survived on bagels and spaghetti while I struggled to complete my bachelor's degree.

That night I dreamed I was on a ride, soaring high above an amusement park.

Everything seemed fine until Bob shifted position in an attempt to involve himself in something that was none of his business. He appeared unconcerned about safety as he moved closer to the edge. The ride leaned toward one side. I felt the tremendous weight of Bob's body when I grabbed his arm and prevented him from falling to his death.

When I awoke I felt tired and decided to remain in bed. I drifted off reflecting on Bob's impulsivity and the dream continued.

At first, I was gliding high above the ground, held aloft by a gust of wind. When the scene changed I found myself at a dance attended by demanding senior citizens. My mother-in-law was seated at a table, alone. A wall was suddenly transformed into a huge garage door and I found myself outside. I felt apprehensive knowing a fugitive was on the loose after slashing a woman's face. Near the end of the dream I felt myself gliding with my arms and legs spread apart. The sensation was exhilarating.

After the second dream I woke up refreshed.

I was unaware Bob had contacted our Spanish restaurant fiasco friends Arlene and Jack about New Year's Eve plans. Turns out reservations had already been made, but Bob asked if we could join them. Arlene promised to check with the caterer, and when Bob called I agreed to join him only if there was room at the table.

The phone rang again the moment I hung up. Arlene wanted to know what to do. I assured her it was all right to make the reservation if she felt comfortable spending the evening with us. I would have thought both of them would still be reeling from the Spanish restaurant evening. After hanging up I was not sure if I had made the right decision. I was so confused; I really needed to talk with Dr. Adler.

Bob called to find out what time to pick me up New Year's Eve. I insisted that I pick him up. After hanging up, I questioned my motive for agreeing to go in the first place. I rationalized that it was an opportunity to relive a tradition and celebrate with friends. Most of the other pleasures in my life had been extinguished.

New Year's Eve turned out to be enjoyable after all. Bob and I danced for most of the evening and shared a chaste kiss at midnight. I dropped him off at his house and was content to return home alone. My comfortable flannel nightgown and fuzzy slippers waited.

During the night I dreamed a hairy chest pressed against me. The feeling was pleasurable, leaving no doubt about whose chest it was. I decided it was time for a therapy tune-up.

Bob's psychological profile was protected by client-patient confidentiality. However, since intimate details had already been discussed in marriage counseling I hoped there would be more flexibility in what Dr. Adler and I could discuss.

During most of the session I expressed concern for Bob. I related a story about a friend from work. Her diabetic dad had been committed to a psychiatric hospital to have his meds regulated. She had given me the name of his endocrinologist, but Bob refused to make an appointment. Dr. Adler agreed that Bob should be monitoring his glucose levels more closely. However, his psychological problems were a separate issue, he said.

I mentioned a television talk show about divorced couples who still had sex with each other. In one segment a couple divorced for 10-years spoke about getting together on the divorce anniversary.

You were fishing for permission to do the same thing, said Ms. Freud.

Dr. Adler's only comment was, "It sounds like an interesting idea."

During the drive home I reflected on my life without Bob. I enjoyed living alone; I loved not dealing with Bob's instability on a day-to-day basis.

Bob called with an Ernie update. I was delighted to learn Ernie was out of rehab and at home recuperating. Bob was anxious for me to choose a date for us to get together for dinner with the kids.

I promised I would try to make arrangements and get back to him. Bob was too unpredictable to risk a family get-together.

I dreamed my friend Jan and I were at a seaside café accompanied by two continental gentlemen.

Jan wanted to take a picture of all of us, but the men objected. We suspected they were married. During the course of the evening they were called outside. The men were not who we imagined them to be. They were employed by the café. After a while I found myself alone at the table. I saw Bob standing at the corner watching me. Even though he was impeccably dressed and looked very appealing, I hoped he would not approach me. My date returned to the table and led me to the cash register. When he saw his boss he rolled up his sleeves and disappeared. Bob appeared at my side with an open checkbook. The cashier recited the amount of the bill. I requested she take it out of my date's salary. She informed me the boss would not like that and I responded, "It's that or nothing." Bob wrote a check to cover the amount of the bill. I was annoyed by his interference and assumption that I would want him involved. My fists pummeled him.

I awoke with fists tightly clenched, nails digging into palms.

My friend Evelyn and I were anxious to try a new restaurant Michelle and Eric had recommended. Not being part of a couple made frequenting upscale restaurants awkward. My coupled friends often asked why I wouldn't date so-and-so for socializing with them as a twosome.

What did they know about all the jerks and losers out there, pondered Ms. Freud?

After dropping Evelyn off, I became lost in thought. An acquaintance had confided how she often worked through her anger by screaming and cursing while alone in her car. The other drivers may have thought her peculiar, but she found the experience cathartic.

Before long I was consumed with toxic thoughts, losing my sense-of-self, money that disappeared and Bob's involvement with prostitutes. I couldn't forgive. We could never pick up where we left off.

"You sick, perverted piece of shit!" I screamed over and over until my throat became hoarse.

It worked.

CHAPTER THIRTY ONE

I was in a rut. The endless days of schoolwork and trying to keep warm wore on. Evelyn and I decided to brave the bitter cold for a change of pace. She suggested a singles' dance on Long Island, even though we would have to drive one hour each way.

The men there were much older, but the Astaire-like ballroom dancing expertise was wonderful. Ironically, the one man with whom I shared a mutual attraction lived not far from me—and if I hadn't ventured out to that God-forsaken location I would never have met Sam.

At the end of the evening we exchanged telephone numbers. He was a widower and even though he was indeed much older, we would both benefit from this budding friendship.

On another rut filled day, Bea invited me over for dinner. Ernie was still recuperating from surgery and was in the mood for company. I had a feeling Bob would be there—and I was right.

The meal was delicious and the evening pleasant until Bob and Bea disagreed on a trivial matter. The conversation escalated, and he became furious. Ernie shrugged and shook his head, a witness to this scenario many times.

But after I foolishly came to Bea's defense I became the target of Bob's wrath. No longer on the receiving end of his merciless tirade, Bea left the table on the pretense of serving dessert. The episode ended just as quickly as it began. Bea returned to the table carrying a coffee pot. She acted as if nothing had happened while chattering about potentially replacing living room carpeting.

After I thanked her for a wonderful dinner and said "Goodbye," to Ernie, Bob lingered at the door. He wanted me to call so we could get together.

He's got to be kidding, said Ms. Freud.

I used to think if I identified what fueled Bob's anger I could help him deal with it—heal him and ultimately save our marriage. Now that I was becoming more objective I realized there was no rhyme or reason, no pattern or predictability behind Bob's behavior. And even though I now saw him only occasionally, I always felt lousy afterwards.

Sam called the moment I arrived home, but I was in no mood to talk with anyone. I offered a vague excuse, and when I did return his call, we made a date for during the week. I rarely went out on a work night, but he noted that's when the restaurant he had in mind played dance music and so I agreed.

School was always in the front of my mind, and I made an appointment to have my college credits evaluated for graduation. Before Bob and I separated, my advisor insisted I take education courses in addition to fulfilling psychology requirements. I had been adamant about not digressing from my goal of becoming a psychotherapist. Mr. Bell insisted that we never know the twists and turns life takes. If I included education courses I would qualify for a teaching certificate.

He must have been psychic, said Ms. Freud.

I played hooky from evening classes to attend the "self-help" guru John Bradshaw's seminar at Jacob Javits Convention Center. My excitement mounted as I drove across the Manhattan Bridge. I had wanted to see him in person ever since I read his book about healing the "inner child." Once inside the vast auditorium thousands of followers hung on his every word. I found Bradshaw's presence mesmerizing and understood why he had so many devotees.

When he spoke about symbolically marrying our parents, it made perfect sense. My first husband had my dad's personality while Bob was very much like my mother.

Bradshaw explained how in order to survive we become desensitized in destructive relationships. He talked extensively about the "inner child" whose needs were not met and how it's the child who is fighting during a confrontation.

I thought about the times Bob shouted in desperation, "Listen to me! Just listen to me!" I imagined how difficult it must have been growing up with Bea jabbering away and relegating him to a position of lesser importance. By the end of a long evening I felt emotionally drained, but decided the trip to Manhattan was definitely worth the effort.

Thoughts about how to celebrate my college graduation resulted in a decision to have a big party. I loved parties and this would be the mother of all parties. I was not sure of the guest list—but I *was* certain Bob would not be on it.

Later in the week Sam appeared on my doorstep, a bouquet of flowers clenched in one hand. The glow radiating from his smile was infectious.

To my surprise the restaurant he chose was nearby. Of course I immediately suspected an ulterior motive for staying close to home. My suspicions were unfounded. After a pleasant evening, Sam walked me to my door, planted a quick smooch on my lips and promised to call later in the week.

The warmth of my cozy apartment and the sight of the beautiful flowers from Sam brought to mind a refrain from a James Brown song, "I feel good. Da-da-da-da-da-da. So good! Da-da. So fine! Da-da. Da-da-da-da-da."

When the phone rang the next evening I was happy to hear Sam's cheerful voice. He wanted to see me the following evening. I begged off; it was too much, too soon.

Sam did not appear put-off by my rejection. We agreed to talk later in the week. I was afraid of getting close. I had constructed an invisible shield insulating myself from the outside world, but the shield offered no defense against relentless innermost thoughts.

CHAPTER THIRTY TWO

I was once asked if there was a valid reason for Bob's promiscuity —but if anyone had a valid reason to be promiscuous it was me.

Bob always blamed me for being the elephant who never forgets.

You're supposed to forget infidelity, mused Ms. Freud?

Whenever we drove through Manhattan Bob never missed an opportunity to point out street corners where prostitutes strolled. I once questioned him about large scratches on his car's glove box, pointedly suggesting the cause was a hooker's stiletto.

He laughed it off. And when I found a cheap earring on the car floor he offered no explanation; rather he grabbed it out of my hand, rolled down the window and tossed it onto the highway.

The next time Sam called I explained that I was under a lot of pressure and although I enjoyed his company I needed to proceed at a slower pace. After expressing his disappointment Sam confessed that he enjoyed my company and wanted to see me as often as possible.

And if you were being honest with yourself, chided Ms. Freud, you would have admitted you wanted to leave an opportunity to go hunting.

But for what?

The only furniture I brought with me to my new apartment was a bridge table and chairs, the mattress from Michelle's old bed and a battered chest of drawers. Every time I looked for new furniture I found it difficult to finalize the sale.

I had been to one particular showroom where I sat on the same upholstered pieces during each visit. The sales lady would acknowledge me with a nod and a knowing smile. I imagined her thinking I was some kind of head-case who would best be left alone. When I settled into the cushions I envisioned how the new furniture would be a welcome addition.

And I soon realized it wasn't money holding me back. I planned to use a credit card (even though carrying a balance for the first time in my life was unconscionable—and as soon as my teaching position was secure my first priority would be to pay off my credit card debt).

Your reluctance to close any deal was caused by your desire for a return to seeking happily ever after, observed Ms. Freud.

On some level I believed the separation was temporary and as soon as Bob came to his senses I would be moving back to our house. But finally logic prevailed and I signed a furniture purchase agreement.

Bob was ready to talk about some of the issues he had been working on in therapy and requested that I return to couple's counseling. I suggested he continue with Dr. Adler until he was able to talk about all the issues. I was not willing to chance another ride on the merry-go-round from hell.

I dreamed I was living in a large, modern, apartment building.

Water leaked down from the ceiling. I heard an electrical "pop" and saw smoke billowing toward me. I remained calm and dialed 9-1-1 before I grabbed my handbag and fled.

After I awoke, I remembered how good I felt being responsible for myself and nobody else. There was never anyone there for me during a crisis—like when Michelle almost drowned in a swimming pool or when a well-meaning passenger on a train gave her a hard candy and she almost choked to death. I was strong for everyone else. Maybe someday someone would be strong for me.

The winter dragged on and pressure mounted during the final term before graduation.

My assistant principal reminded me about the New York State Board of Education's deadline approaching for completing requirements. I needed to obtain certification in time for her to consider me for a teaching position. During this stressful time the only ray of sunshine came from my wonderful supportive friends and family—and of course, Dr. Adler.

I was consumed with research, followed by endless hours of typing term papers. And no matter how many layers of clothing I wore, it was impossible to warm up. I turned the thermostat off at night to save money on the astronomical heating bill.

When I went to bed I looked like "Nanook of the north," buried under a mountain of blankets and quilts. I drifted off with Teddy clutched tightly, envisioning a time when this part of my life would be a distant memory.

I dreaded having to throw back the covers each morning and then enter the unheated bathroom. To turn up the heat in the apartment on a workday did not make sense. By the time I finished washing, dressing and eating a sparse breakfast the apartment would just be warming up.

I complained about my heating predicament to Mel when we were clearing a path to the curb after a snowfall. He suggested I purchase an electric heater and keep it in the bathroom. He reminded me to keep it unplugged when not in use. Mel was right. The heater's radiance filled the tiny room in seconds and I was able to complete my morning ritual with a newfound enthusiasm.

A tremendous amount of snow fell over the weekend followed by partial melting and then an unexpected dip in temperature. By Monday morning there was a sheet of ice everywhere.

In order to reach the front of the house I held on to the fence along the length of the building and cautiously, hand-over-hand, I made my way to the front gate. When I arrived at my car I found all four tires encased in ice. I struggled to the bus stop on the corner and waited with my back pressed against the wall for wind protection.

During staff lunch period everyone swapped stories about the icy, early morning adventures. When it was my turn I confessed that I did not have a clue how to extricate ice-bound tires.

Co-worker Jim came to my rescue. "Before you head home stop at the hardware store and buy an ice chopper with a long handle. Slowly chip away at the ice and be very careful not to puncture a tire." I was so grateful for his advice I wanted to kiss him.

But you restrained yourself, smiled Ms. Freud.

As the newly educated winter warrior, I boarded the bus later that afternoon with an ice chopper in hand. As we rode I envisioned a conquest over the ice and with Jim's words echoing in my ears, I rallied forth to eliminate the enemy.

Spurred on by a belief that if I conquered the elements I would also surmount life's current and future obstacles, I spent the better part of an hour chipping away and sculpting an escape path.

It was a beautiful thing—and a reassuring belief.

CHAPTER THIRTY THREE

My car was broken into while at work. My first thought was how Bob would react.

And how sick was that, asked Ms. Freud?

However, the insurance arrangement with Bob made secrecy impossible. I didn't go into detail on the phone, and we agreed to meet for breakfast the following day.

After being seated Bob handed me two pink envelopes. I had completely forgotten about Valentine's Day.

In the first envelope was a card for Michelle. I was relieved to find the second envelope contained a humorous card for me that did not mention love. I pretended not to notice the long, white envelope also on the table.

I thanked Bob for both cards and got down to business. When I described the damaged car, Bob's anger wasn't loud, but it was obvious.

"Why don't you watch where you park?"

"I would if I had a choice, but I don't when I'm at work."

He quickly changed the subject, saying he had been burglarized twice after I moved out. The items he reported stolen included:

1. A fur jacket I had left behind.
2. A fur coat that may have been his mother's outdated mink.

3. My diamond engagement and wedding rings (which were in fact in my possession).

4. A Monte Blanc pen I didn't know he owned.

5. And a Patek Phillipe watch that had belonged to his father.

The second reported break-in took place in the padlocked garage behind the house.

He's a liar and opportunist, said Ms. Freud, and he'd have no problem filing a police report, submitting an insurance claim and expecting everybody to believe his story.

However, I could no longer contain my curiosity. "So what's in the envelope?" I asked, detecting the flick of tongue across his lips and a grin that said, "gotcha!"

Bob removed two checks and placed them in front of me. Each represented settlements under our homeowner's insurance policy. But I suspected he had filed false claims, and when I looked and realized the checks were payable to both of us I went into a full panic mode.

I shouted across the table. "How did you think you would get away with this? You must have signed my name to the police reports and the insurance claims!"

He offered nothing in the way of explanation or rebuttal. It was obvious the ramifications of his actions never crossed his mind. Where was his conscience? Bob was focused on only one thing—getting his hands on the money. To lecture him further would have been futile.

He was matter-of-fact. "If you endorse the checks, I'll share the money with you."

"Your offer is very generous, but I need time to think it over," I responded. "In the meantime the insurance company has to be notified about my car and you have all the policy information."

Bob agreed to call the insurance company that afternoon and I promised to get back to him regarding the checks.

He's truly clueless if he thinks you're going to participate in his deception, argued Ms. Freud.

All I thought about driving home was Bob's unmitigated gall if he expected me to participate. Even if the settlement was for $1 million, I would not have been tempted.

But I had to stop thinking about it because Michelle and I were going on vacation to Florida. The original plan was to travel in coach, but Amtrak was offering a deal on sleeping accommodations.

What the hell—upgrade, said Ms. Freud.

There would be one more expense on my charge account and I looked forward to a pajama party where Michelle would share my enthusiasm for adventure on the rails. I imagined snuggling in a sleeper car, the rhythmic clatter as the train passed over the railroad ties, "click-clack, click-clack," and a solitary train whistle wailing in the darkness.

But for Michelle the train ride turned out to be a very bad experience. She found the continuous motion and the relentless noise a sensory assault. But she agreed later that the balance of the vacation compensated for the initial discomfort. The sun's warmth and the crystal-clear ocean were glorious and finding my dad and step-dad in relatively good health indeed made the long train ride worthwhile.

The apartment felt like a sauna when I returned; the thermostat had gone haywire. The only person I could think of to ask for help was Bob. Reluctantly, I called. He had a sample thermostat and promised to come right over.

I marveled at how quickly he completed the job. After he explained the operating instructions and opened the windows, he suggested we go to dinner while the apartment cooled down. All during dinner I waited for him to mention the insurance checks, but he never did. We talked about my trip and how the kids were doing.

You know he signed your name to those checks and cashed them, said Ms. Freud.

Adding to my burgeoning charge account, I continued to nurse my sickly car. But I felt entitled to something special—a reward for keeping my nose to the grindstone.

I had been admiring a luxurious leather jacket in a store window for some time, but it was too expensive. I decided to put it on my charge account. The jacket would be symbolic of the struggle—and ultimately my success.

CHAPTER THIRTY FOUR

Whenever I felt upbeat something occurred to dispel the good mood.

The bathroom ceiling started to leak again and I received a whopping dental bill. Fortunately my savior Sam called to ask me out Saturday night. After I hung up, I fell into a fitful sleep and a dream played out in a succession of vignettes.

I was riding a tricycle through country roads. I stopped for repairs and two children stopped to help me. Then, I was kidnapped by a friendly man and woman. The country setting changed to palm trees.

This segment was followed by a brief view of a phallic symbol. The dream continued with me being invited to a wedding.

I didn't like my dress so I removed it. Bob was with me and for a while he appeared normal. That was until he removed his jacket to reveal three shirts, one on top of the other, all hanging outside his pants.

Will your dreams about Bob ever cease, Ms. Freud wondered?

Sam appeared at my door Saturday holding flowers. We enjoyed another pleasant evening—a lovely dinner followed by a musical performance at Brooklyn College. The night ended with a smooch.

News about my upcoming graduation had spread among co-workers. The gifts and cards which followed all appreciated my accomplishment.

Sam presented me with a tape recorder. He thought it would be helpful when I started teaching. It was such a lovely gesture. My gratitude was genuine but there was something unsettling about the gift. I felt the tape recorder represented the beginning of a serious relationship. Sam was a dear sweet man, but he was so much older.

Sam attended the World's Fair with his children the year you were born, sighed Ms. Freud, and that definitely means friends only.

I tried my best to discourage Sam, but he insisted there was promise in my eyes. I made a joke about not realizing that I had such a powerful influence. He just laughed and told me he had found what he wanted in me.

His expectations were unrealistic. I recommended a nice woman closer to his age. Reluctantly, Sam accepted the phone number and promised to report back.

Driving home after my evening classes proved to be a harrowing experience. The temperature had dropped below freezing and the weather report warned of treacherous black ice. I felt a tremendous surge of anger. I should have been in a nice warm house instead of sliding around on an icy road.

And if Bob was normal, Ms. Freud sighed, you wouldn't be back in the dating rat-race.

I thought about a television interview I had seen where a woman shot her ex-husband and his new wife. The ex-wife claimed that for years she was subjected to mental abuse until one day she just snapped.

Her story reminded me of the Christmas before I moved out, and when the kids had given us a stainless steel cutlery set. I had placed the wooden block containing the knives on the kitchen counter.

I would often glance at the knives during heated encounters and think how gratified I would feel after plunging a knife through Bob's heart, putting an end to his craziness. Thankfully I recognized that this momentary loss of control would herald the beginning of my own mental instability.

It was another cold blustery day, the kind that made me want to stay in bed instead of trudging off to work. However, the luxury of remaining in bed whenever the mood struck was a long way off.

Later in the day the temperature warmed up considerably. I was unaware that the drain in front of my apartment door had been blocked by ice. When the snow began to melt there was no place for the water to go but in under the door.

I discovered the shallow pond just inside the door when I arrived home after work. It only took a moment to understand what had occurred. Another person would have assessed the damage and immediately begin the task of cleaning up the mess, but at that moment I was unable to deal with it. Instead, I closed the door and walked two blocks to the neighborhood pizzeria where I ordered a slice with everything, and a very large glass of Chianti. Only after I was sufficiently fortified was I able to tackle the disaster.

Bob and I had an appointment with our accountant. In years past I had felt like a child accompanying a parent. Bob usually gathered our financial records and did all the talking while I remained mute. I was becoming aware that not paying closer attention had been a mistake. I promised myself this time would be different.

Before I signed the tax return I attempted to ask a question. Bob cut me off claiming he was in a hurry. I glanced over at the accountant hoping he would say something, but he had already turned his attention to the huge pile of tax returns on his desk. The dutiful child signed on the dotted line. On the way out Bob suggested we discuss things over dinner.

We drove to a restaurant where the lighting was dim and the music ideal for dancing cheek-to-cheek. It was not exactly the setting I would have chosen for a financial discussion or a therapy session. I had a number of unanswered questions about our finances and Bob's indiscretions, but Bob twisted my words until my inquiries made me sound paranoid.

I brought up the night in Quebec when he left me in our hotel room and didn't return for hours. He had an answer for everything. He reminded me that he had asked if I wanted to accompany him on his late night tour, but I declined. Of course I declined. We had been sightseeing all day, it was 11 p.m. and I was exhausted.

"I can't ignore your infidelity."

Bob was flustered. "What should I do? What do you want me to say? I'm sorry—OK? I'm sorry. I don't understand why you can't put this all in the past and just move on."

"Wasn't I enough for you?"

"It's not you. You know that."

"Please—I've heard that before."

"I've always been attracted to—to ethnic woman. It goes back to when I delivered mattresses for my father..." Bob's voice trailed off as his eyes glazed over.

"A lot of our clientele lived in walk-up buildings. They were mostly women home alone. Sometimes there were young children sleeping in the next room. I made the deliveries myself and by the time I dragged a mattress up all those stairs I was worn out. They couldn't tip—they were poor."

He hesitated.

"Don't stop now," I implored. "Finish what you were saying."

"They offered me a cold drink. Sometimes they made enticing remarks."

And you envisioned a strong young buck of a man, said Ms. Freud, leaning against the doorway breathing heavily, moist with perspiration.

Bob struggled to continue.

"The women would ask if there was anything else they could offer me. And that's how it began."

Even if Bob repeated the Holy Rosary there would not have been enough Hail Marys to absolve him of all sins.

Asked Ms. Freud: Is your inability to move past these issues more about your father cheating on your mother than with what happened with Bob?

I had difficulty understanding how Bob professed love for me and at the same time he had destroyed everything in our lives that was meaningful.

But you were certain of one thing, chuckled Ms. Freud—you were still hot for him.

Bob asked if I would sleep over and I agreed. When we made love Bob's performance felt mechanical, as if he were following a checklist, making sure not to skip an item lest he receive an unfavorable review. Once I was able to set my observations aside, I responded to the moment with abandon.

The next morning I was greeted by the old Bob. He had been up early, busily preparing breakfast. He even offered to serve me in bed. The aroma of bacon and eggs, French toast and coffee wafted up from the kitchen.

From the extensive menu it was obvious Bob was trying hard to please me. He indicated where I should sit and proceeded to pour coffee. We separated the newspaper into sections and recited articles of interest while we ate. I speculated on what the SWF in the personals really looked like. We joked and laughed until he abruptly stopped.

My sense of dread displaced the pleasure felt up until that moment. I braced for what was to come.

Bob began rambling about attending an antique show with friend's who shared our interest in collecting Japanese pottery—and before I had a chance to comment his plan changed: he now believed the day would prove exhausting and suggested we stay in a hotel overnight.

I opened my mouth to speak, but the plan changed again.

Bob wanted to extend the stay over a weekend. He jumped up, hurried out of the kitchen and returned with his attaché case. He was already extremely agitated when he handed me a brochure offering a discount for a two-night stay.

After glancing at the literature I told Bob the hotel seemed fine. Not satisfied he snarled, "Give that to me!" and abruptly pulled the brochure from my hand.

After rummaging through some papers Bob removed yet another brochure and with trembling hands, thrust it toward me. This hotel was more expensive than the first one. I pointed out that the price included meals and entertainment and I didn't think regimentation would be a good idea.

I was certain he would crack under the pressure if deciding where to stay created such turmoil. My thoughts were interrupted by the sound of him slamming the attaché case shut.

"Well, do you want to stay in the first place or the second place?" he asked angrily.

As if his indecisiveness is your fault, remarked Ms. Freud.

I pointed out that he was angry because he was unable to make a decision. He continued to blame me and insisted he was only reacting to my anger.

I felt the merry-go-round yet again in motion but I chose not to ride this day. As I walked toward the door, Bob yelled after me, "You don't have to run away! Don't go."

"Nice while it lasted," I called over my shoulder. "With you it's not a matter of *if* the shoe will fall, but *when* the shoe will fall. You forget I don't live here anymore. I can go home."

Free will—and how liberating is that, smiled Ms. Freud.

CHAPTER THIRTY FIVE

I had thought much about how I would celebrate the momentous occasion of my college graduation—and was certain of only one thing: Bob would not be on the guest list.

Bea had offered to make me a graduation party, but I was sure the only reason was to be sure I invited her sonny-boy. And even if she was sincere, her involvement would make a great situation awkward.

Over the years I had attended other people's surprise parties. I waited in vain for my surprise, but it never came. I never had a Sweet Sixteen, baby or wedding shower, or 40th or 50th birthday party.

You deserved to be honored, Ms. Freud said, and the only way to insure that was to do it for yourself.

Since I was fired up about my own party I also decided to plan something special for my dad's 75th birthday. I spoke to my brother about gathering at a resort in the Catskill Mountains. When my dad visited during the summer we would drive up with Michelle and Eric; my brother would fly in directly and surprise Dad. After Larry agreed to the plan I could barely contain my excitement.

I danced with the DJ, Vinny at a church social. Vinny was very smooth. He said and did all the right things and made me feel like a teenager. I had a great time even though I was wary of Mr. Wonderful.

During the evening he was approached by several women. As he pecked each on the cheek I detected a wistful longing in the lady's eyes. Vinny had been single for many years and it was conceivable he had banged every woman at every dance he had ever hosted. I didn't care; I was having the most fun I have had in a long time and I planned on going home the same way I arrived, alone.

The next morning I was still glowing from the previous evening. I stopped to pick up the Sunday newspaper and headed out for a hearty breakfast. When I arrived at the Oasis, Bob was seated at the counter. We acknowledged each other with a nod and I proceeded to a booth at the rear. When I looked up from my newspaper Bob was standing beside the table. He appeared disheveled, disoriented and stumbled over his words.

"There's something—some mail for you. At the house—there's mail."

I promised to stop by but wanted to relax first and was not sure what time I would be there. Bob sounded annoyed when I suggested he leave the mail behind the unlocked screen door. He walked away in a huff.

I thought it best to pick up the mail before he had a "hissy" fit and trashed it. When I opened the screen door the squeaking hinges alerted him. He appeared in the entranceway and beckoned me to come inside.

Piles of newspapers and plastic bags were strewn everywhere. The scene was reminiscent of the stories I had read about the Collyer brothers. The brothers died surrounded by 130 tons of waste.

And instead of handing over the mail, Bob offered a jumbled explanation of capital gains—and if we did not get back together how that pertained to the house sale.

"Do you think I give a crap about capital gains when you live here while I barely exist in a room?"

"Whose fault is that? I never wanted you to leave."

"You forced me out!" I shrieked, holding back tears.

"You didn't have to leave," Bob's voice cracked when he spoke. "I never wanted this—I never wanted us to break up."

"How could you not understand that we had already broken up when I moved into the other bedroom?" I asked incredulously.

I did not mention that I had consulted with a lawyer and I planned to file for divorce in the fall. Bob handed me the mail and I left feeling angry at myself for being lured into another hopeless dialogue.

And as the graduation party approached, I won the New York Lottery.

Yep, you really did, laughed Ms. Freud.

It was not exactly the jackpot, but it sure felt like it. The *Take Five Quick Pick* paid $522 for four correct numbers. I was excited until I remembered the upcoming party and the weekend I planned for my dad. I had no choice but to deposit the money in my piddling savings account.

After researching places for the graduation party I reserved a private room in a restaurant/lounge. We would be close enough to hear the band play and still maintain privacy. Michelle volunteered to host the party, mail out invitations and keep track of the RSVP's.

Sam called to report on his recent date. He wanted to know how I could possibly think he would be interested in such a person. She was nothing like me. He wanted me to reconsider my decision and continue to date him. He was such a darling man.

If only he were younger, sighed Ms. Freud.

We did enjoy each other's company and we both loved to dance. He accepted my offer to be his dancing partner and our relationship continued, minus the floral bouquets.

Bob was in a foul mood when next he called to let me know his glucose monitor had broken. It was imperative that he monitor his blood throughout the day. Knowing Bob, the last reading must have been too high and he threw the device across the room in a fit of anger.

"I don't know what to do—I need it right away." He sounded frantic.

I assured him I would contact the insurance company and find out the proper procedure. Within an hour an emergency order was placed and Bob was instructed to pick up a new glucose monitor from a medical supply distributor.

Several of my co-workers were graduating with me, and I learned each had not attended a high school prom. We thought it would be a hoot to see expressions on faces of the younger graduates when a group of adults showed up at the prom.

Michelle picked me up in the midst of a torrential rainstorm. I was touched by her thoughtfulness when she brought a beautiful corsage. By the time we arrived at the college I had to remove my shoes before running to the gymnasium. The cool rainwater on my feet was exhilarating.

Our group was the hit of the evening. We were young enough to keep up with the music and old enough to arouse curiosity. The faculty dispatched an emissary to inquire who we were. I was certain the motive was to learn what was in the brown paper bags we were hiding under the table. There was more than enough wine to go around. We offered to share our "stash" with our new best friends— the faculty.

In making the guest list for the graduation party I reflected on which people had touched my life in a positive way. I thought back to when I had a crush on a married co-worker. I believed the attraction was mutual although neither of us ever acted on the feelings.

Leo had been my confidant, my mentor, always encouraging me to continue my education or establish my own business. Apparently he recognized my potential when nobody else did. I was curious about what he would think of me now. I wondered if the old spark would be there.

When I checked the telephone directory Leo was living at his old address. I could feel my face flush with anticipation as I wrote out his invitation.

My dad was a man of few words, but he never failed to pick out the most sentimental greeting cards. He expressed his heartfelt congratulations for my achievement and enclosed a $500 check. On a separate slip of yellow paper was a message printed in block letters.

Dear Lee,

Enclosed you will find a check for $500 which you very much deserve.

Love, Daddy

I began to cry. Everything I had thought or felt about myself was validated by dad's words.

He never knew how much you needed to hear that, said Ms. Freud.

UPS delivered an adorable Vermont Teddy Bear, dressed like a graduate in a cap and gown and holding a tiny diploma. When I realized the gift was from Leo I felt let down. I thought it meant he would not be attending.

Leo called before I had a chance to call. We spoke for a long time. He told me he loved talking to me. The feeling was mutual and I believed the bond we once shared still existed.

He confessed he held off responding to the invitation because he was trying to lose some weight before seeing me. He didn't know I had always been a chubby-chaser. Although I had never met his wife I included her in the invitation. Leo said she had not been feeling well and he would be attending the party without her.

Leo ended the conversation by calling me "sweetie," and when I hung up my heart was singing.

CHAPTER THIRTY SIX

To my surprise and delight everyone accepted the graduation party invitation—including Dr. Adler. The night of the party I attached a balloon on each graduate's chair and included those names on the special occasion cake.

Michelle surprised me by placing a single long-stemmed rose next to each place setting. She was the perfect hostess, greeting each guest and placing gifts on a side table. This was all the parties I never had rolled into one.

It was the best party in the history of the world, smiled Ms. Freud.

At the end of the evening it became clear the crush Leo and I once shared would remain part of our past. He had always been faithful to his wife and that was not going to change. He did promise to stay in touch. We continued to talk until Leo called my attention to the late hour. We embraced and kissed as if lovers reunited after a long absence.

Shortly after the graduation party, I received a lovely letter from Dr. Adler which read in part:

"The feeling of being at your graduation party is very difficult to put into words. It was certainly a thrilling experience, with the additional excitement, which you were clearly experiencing. While the last months have been difficult for you, I hope that this event proves to be the start of the most significant phase of your life. For your generous sharing of your experience, my thanks."

After the prom and party, the graduation ceremony itself felt anticlimactic. The sun shone with an unforgiving ferocity as students lined up along the stone walkway leading from the college cafeteria. Everyone was experiencing varying degrees of discomfort under polyester graduation gowns.

Perspiration slithered down our bodies as the procession moved toward the staging area. My eyes blurred with tears when I reflected on the hardships I had endured to reach this milestone.

How proud everyone felt—how proud you felt, said Ms. Freud.

After the speeches and presentations, the long, hot graduation day finally ended. Earlier Michelle and Eric wanted me to choose a post graduation ceremony restaurant. I requested my favorite Spanish restaurant—where Bob had thrown a fit and walked out leaving me sitting with our friends.

I breathed an it's-finally-over sigh of relief as we drove to that restaurant for the celebratory dinner. We waited in the garden until a table was ready. The sound of water splashing from a weathered, stone fountain onto the cobblestones below had a restorative effect. I thought about how uncomplicated the day had been without having to contend with Bob's mood swings.

Graduation was followed by the long awaited celebration of my father's 75th birthday. The surprise my brother Larry and I planned worked out perfectly. Larry and his girlfriend Pam arrived from the airport in the hotel's courtesy van. At first my dad appeared confused when he saw them walking toward him.

"Oh my God, I can't believe this. How did you get here?"

"We were in the neighborhood!" my brother quipped.

It warmed my heart to see Dad enjoy himself. He ate with gusto and even participated in a ping-pong tournament. We took long walks and reminisced about the piggyback rides he gave me when I was younger—and long after I had reached a comfortable piggyback riding weight.

After the nightclub entertainment Saturday night many guests retired for the evening; others headed toward a coffee shop for a late night snack. But for the hail and hearty whose mission it was to take full advantage of every activity offered, the highlight of the weekend was the "Battle of the Sexes."

At first my dad was reluctant to stay up past midnight, but when we explained the competition was between a male and a female "dancer" in an intimate lounge, he became energized and assured us he was capable of staying up as late as necessary. His only concern was that Roberta would find out. We swore not to say a word.

Dad maintained composure. While everyone else was hooting and hollering, he declined the opportunity to place folded dollar bills in the dancers' "G" strings. That was until the buxom female "dancer" plopped down on his lap.

Hugh Hefner would not have been more delighted, smiled Ms. Freud.

On the morning we were scheduled to return home I emerged from the steamy bathroom draped in terrycloth and found Dad cradling his head in hands. For a moment I panicked. Oh my God, he ate the wrong foods. Exerted himself too much? Was the late show too strenuous?

When I approached the bed I heard him stifle a cry. When I put a hand on his shoulder, he quickly wiped his eyes and appeared embarrassed.

"Dad, what's the matter? Are you all right?"

"I'm fine, really I'm fine."

"You can't be fine. It's obvious that something is upsetting you. Are you sick? Should I call the front desk and request a doctor?"

"Look what you made me do. My whole life I never cried." A sob caught in his throat.

"Sometimes crying is a good thing. It means you're getting in touch with your feelings," I replied.

"Why did you kids do this for me? I cheated on your mother—I don't deserve this. You and your brother had a hard life because of me. Who you are, and everything you did, you accomplished without me."

His voice trailed off as he attempted to regain composure.

"Do you believe you are so unlovable?" I asked. "Should you be punished for the rest of your life? Haven't you been punished enough? Larry and I forgive you; now it's time to forgive yourself."

He nodded and reached out to hug me. I was reminded of the times he had comforted me as a child and rescued me when my mother lashed out with hurtful words. I never understood until years later that her anger was misdirected.

CHAPTER THIRTY SEVEN

During that same weekend my dad inquired if I would consider moving to a larger apartment. This was the first time he mentioned my inadequate living arrangement, but it must have upset him to see me living in a tiny apartment while Bob lived in our house.

However, the only difference between a studio and a one-bedroom was the door that separated the rooms—and the one-bedroom rent was significantly higher.

You had better things to do with your money, said Ms. Freud.

I saw his disappointment after I explained how I felt. I also felt relieved when he chose not to argue the point.

On the drive home, I glanced at his tranquil face. He had fallen into a peaceful slumber. I would always love this man no matter what. He was my Dad, after all—and I hoped he would never forget the incredible four days we shared as a family.

When I returned home there was a message from Bea. She accepted that Bob and I might never get back together, but she would continue to encourage him to see a psychiatrist for medication.

Imagine that, sighed Ms. Freud.

On the education front, my principal advised me about a teaching license application backlog at the State Education Department in Albany. Applications had to be received by the end of the term or processing would be delayed until after the summer. I would not be considered for a teaching position in time for the fall term unless I hand-delivered my paperwork to Albany before the deadline, she said.

I was not capable of driving a great distance to an unfamiliar destination without a navigator. I needed someone to guide me or I would feel like I was driving to a foreign country. I knew I could not negotiate the highways and follow directions by myself.

If I asked Bob to accompany me knowing how unstable he was, I would be leaving myself open for a potentially disastrous experience. I had no choice; I was desperate. Besides, nothing he did would surprise me. I had experienced it all before. Once my official business was completed I would have no qualms about dropping him off at the nearest Greyhound bus terminal.

To my surprise, the drive to Albany went smoothly except for Bob's constant fidgeting. During his sporadic attempts at conversation I found myself on guard, watching for the inevitable Bob changes. By the time we arrived it was obvious Bob was on his way to a major mood swing. I sensed it in the tone of his voice and the way he walked. His whole demeanor warned of an impending emotional storm.

We entered the grand hallway at the education department sounding like two harnessed plow horses, footsteps resounding through the cavernous hallways. When I signed in at the reception area I learned there would be at least an hour wait.

At first Bob sat beside me and continued to fidget. I doubted whether he was capable of waiting that length of time. Bob confided that he was experiencing emotional, as well as physical distress. I suggested he develop coping skills unless he planned to live like a hermit the rest of his life.

He paced back and forth across the room at a dizzying pace until I insisted he explore the vast complex of state government buildings while he waited. He thought that was a good idea because he wanted to do everything in his power to have a pleasant day. I was relieved when he left the office, but I was still tempted to drop him off at the bus terminal on the way home.

Whenever I was with Bob I felt conflicted. There was an element of familiarity and longing. After each encounter I would be reminded that I was still in love with him despite how destructive our relationship had been. The good times were wonderful, but the pain of betrayal and the constant fear of Bob's instability were always present.

But today's disappointment didn't involve Bob, said Ms. Freud.

After I was ushered into the interviewer's office, he informed me that the college had failed to include the last page of my transcript. I had carried the sealed envelope as if it were a priceless treasure and had driven all the way to Albany for nothing. I was advised to return and pick up the correct documentation, potentially delaying the certification process even further.

When I looked at my watch and realized Bob would be waiting outside, my resolve shattered and I broke down crying. Through sobs I heard the interviewer's attempts to console me. I explained that I needed to file paperwork before the deadline or I would miss out on the job I had been promised. My personal life tumbled out along with dreading I would have Bob to contend with once I departed.

The interviewer suggested that after I retrieve the missing page I send the complete transcript via express mail and he would make sure it was processed in a timely fashion. I knew how hard he was trying to help, but his soothing voice and outpouring of kindness would not quell feelings of helplessness and despair and I cried even harder.

By the time I left the office my nerves were so frazzled I imagined someone hiding in the public rest room.

Talk about not having coping skills, chided Ms. Freud. Where in hell were yours?

And now my anxiety had manifested into paranoia. I was unable to concentrate and was too rattled from the day's events. Bob volunteered to drive.

At first I hesitated. The memory of him almost driving off the road on a previous occasion flashed through my mind. It hadn't been that long ago that he nearly killed us swerving to avoid one of his hallucinations.

Nonetheless you accepted his offer, Ms. Freud said—and recited a silent prayer.

During the long ride Bob's expression of remorse was touching. He missed me very much and although therapy was a very painful process he was beginning to realize how his actions destroyed our marriage. This was accompanied by acknowledgement that he needed serious medication.

Actions speak louder than words, mumbled Ms. Freud.

I drifted off to sleep.

I felt relaxed when Bob woke me at a rest stop some two hours later. I could also tell he was relieved when I offered to resume driving. The day had been difficult for both of us, and I was so happy when I finally arrived at the peace and quiet of my, albeit, tiny sanctuary. There I found Teddy bear, and sanity.

A huge sigh of relief came over me after the correct documentation was finally on its way to Albany. I celebrated by having my ears pierced for a second set of earrings. I dubbed the new holes "Freedom" holes, as each would remind me of the escape from my previous life.

PART FIVE

THE BRASS RING IN SIGHT

CHAPTER THIRTY EIGHT

When I was invited for dinner some time later, Bea assured me Bob would not be joining us. I wondered if she and Ernie were feeling lonely, or if this was just keeping communication lines open.

And although you had great affection for Bea, Ms. Freud observed, she betrayed you. She should have revealed more about Bob's mental illness before you were married.

But I appreciated the invitation and Bob's name was never mentioned during dinner.

I arranged to meet my friend Sylvia for lunch. I looked forward to our lively conversations and over the summer our friendship blossomed. Eventually we shared our life experiences. I was looking forward to the next phase of my life. Sylvia assured me one day we would look back on this time and laugh. She had made it through unscathed and so would I.

Intellectually I understood my marriage was over, but I still felt pain—not for what was, but for what may have been. Emotionally I still felt a strong connection to Bob. I was looking for someone to help me break that connection, to share my future. That person would have to be secure enough to not be jealous of my relationship with my daughter. He would have to be honest and sensitive.

And above all else—sane, demanded Ms. Freud. No anger No screaming. No blaming. No mood swings. No nothing!

I always thought we were supposed to have someone to grow old with, someone to comfort us—to soothe us if we became sick or disabled. This was not the way it was supposed to be. I dreaded the thought of hunting for a significant other at this stage of my life.

Stories emerged about what "the sick one" had said about me, or altercations involving other people. Friends and relatives never mentioned these incidents while Bob and I were together.

And if you had known about those things sooner, Ms. Freud said, you would have understood that your struggle to hide everything was futile—and maybe dealt with everything sooner and saved yourself a lot of grief.

I found one particular story most interesting. Bob had a habit of gazing over a person's shoulder when he spoke to them, particularly when we were at the beach club. Our friends often asked what he was staring at.

Although Bob never responded, he often looked like a kid caught with his hand in the cookie jar whenever this behavior was brought to his attention. Eventually I learned Bob was attracted to a mutual female acquaintance, and with whom a flirtation had been going on for quite some time.

The summer turned out to be a downer. There was a lot of rain and I had to deal with my first flat tire—and I think the weather brought out all the weirdoes.

You were also having two answering machine relationships, Ms. Freud laughed—giving new meaning to safe sex.

I looked forward to regaining control of my life, earning a master's degree, traveling abroad, possibly becoming a grandparent and giving the greatest gift I had to give.

Yourself, said Ms. Freud, and to someone who was worthy.

It had been a long time since I attended a Wednesday matinee in Manhattan. It was 25 minutes before curtain-time and I was feeling mellow. I had just finished a robust glass of Merlot and a shrimp cocktail in the luxurious surroundings of the Marriott Marquis Hotel.

While I sipped a steaming cup of black coffee, I reflected on my last attempt to attend the theatre with Bob in tow. He had difficulty sitting still during the performance, getting up more than once to go to the bathroom and eventually receiving a scathing reprimand from an elderly woman sitting in front of us.

On the way home the express bus hurtled through the city. I pressed my nose to the window and watched familiar streets race by. I had enjoyed a wonderful day without Bob weighing me down.

I tried to remember when I first noticed his peculiar behavior. Early in our marriage I became alarmed at what I believed to be his "split personality" when he often referred to himself as "we." There were times during love-making Bob's voice changed dramatically and I was certain he had morphed into another being.

It was as if Bob compartmentalized different aspects of his personality, but when he was stressed or angry or in the throes of passion, another persona emerged. I once called the psychiatrist Bob had introduced me to before we were married to ask if Bob was dangerous. Dr. Oliver's answer was, "only to himself."

I no longer felt intense anger during waking hours and the aggression I once expressed in dreams dissipated.

I enjoyed another leisurely day exploring the streets of Manhattan, eating lunch at "Peppermint Park" and browsing the art show in Washington Square Park. Bob and I had looked forward to the event every year—but usually with disastrous results.

And I hoped I would not encounter Bob when I attended a neighborhood dance later with friends, but no sooner had we entered the ballroom Bob swooped down. His attempt at conversation was awkward, but I tried my best to sound cordial.

Bob asked me to dance. I thought of the possible consequences if I rejected him. The song was almost over when I nodded my head in acceptance.

The music ended, I mumbled "thank you" and quickly retreated into the crowd. Throughout the evening I found myself gazing across the crowded dance floor, searching faces for some sign of Bob. When our eyes finally met, sadness and longing washed over me. We kept our distance for the rest of the evening.

CHAPTER THIRTY NINE

I was under the impression that after my college transcript was approved I would begin teaching when the term started.

Nope, said Ms. Freud. You should have known better.

There are always additional complications and obstacles. My principal explained that graduates would continue as teaching assistants until receiving new ID numbers from the Board of Education. She suggested we remain patient and remember that students were the first priority.

I mentally noted my current dilemma: Credit card maxed out. Clunker of a car on death's door. Cutting napkins in half. Relying on the college cafeteria for packets of condiments.

But you had a steady job, a roof over your head and dick-head out of your life, so you decided to chill, said Ms. Freud.

Before I fell asleep, I had been thinking about the weekend Larry and I spent with our dad. That resulted in an invitation to Larry to visit. I envisioned having fun and acting like kids again—but this time would be different.

He would share my tiny space, but would not have to concern himself with Bob's threats if he forgot to clean up his toast crumbs after breakfast. When Larry related such an incident with Bob shortly after Bob and I separated, he confessed that thereafter he took a silent oath never to stay in our house.

At work, and on one of the mandated half-days where staff had afternoon workshops, I planned to have lunch with Sandy and Laura. Each was always eager to hear my continuing saga.

I was grateful for those friendships. In a previous conversation, Sandy had enlightened me to a chameleon-like personality she referred to as the "salesman's personality." Unable to work and play well with others, a large percentage of these people choose a career in outside sales, Sandy said.

And your chameleon Bob acted charming and ingratiating one moment, agreed Ms. Freud, and followed by everyone ducking for cover the next moment.

Sandy's comments triggered a torrent of emotion. I thought about how I wound up in my predicament and wondered if I was attracted to people with emotional problems because I felt comfortable in that environment?

Did those eccentricities remind me of when I experienced my family's instability? Or did I fancy myself a mental health professional in training? Friends and co-workers relied on me for advice, knowing that whatever I was told would be held in strict confidence. Whether my advice was followed wasn't important; just knowing someone felt better after talking to me gave me satisfaction.

Dancing had always been a tonic for whatever ailed me. It left me feeling euphoric. If I needed a lift, dancing raised my spirits. If work was not going well, dancing was my escape.

My friend Laura shared this perspective, particularly when it came to the Friday night dance we referred to as "The Zoo." This dance attracted all kinds of characters. Anyone entering the dimly lit ballroom would be struck by this group's diversity. If a Hollywood director held a casting call for ballroom types, this crowd would have shown up.

There was always a huge crowd which we attributed to live music, accessible parking, and Friday night infamously known as cheater's night. These sleaze balls usually congregated at the far end of the ballroom, near the bar. The cheaters were not so much interested in dancing as in hooking up.

One exceptionally warm Friday night I wandered over to the bar to get a diet soda. A young man began the usual single's dialogue:

"Have you been here before? How come such a nice gal like you doesn't have a boyfriend?"

I was impressed with the young man when he offered to pay for my drink. He asked me to dance, but instead of moving onto the dance floor we danced near the bar. I cautiously searched for signs of impropriety—and then noticed tin-foil peeking out of his shirt pocket.

I abruptly ceased dancing and pushed him away—but not before grabbing one of the tin foil packets and shaking it menacingly.

The damn arrogance, you thought, said Ms. Freud.

"You must be very sure of yourself if you carry your condoms in plain sight," I fumed. "I suppose your motto is 'Always Be Prepared'—but you don't look like a Boy Scout to me!"

As I continued the irrational ramble it became obvious from his incredulous expression the man thought he had found a mad woman. Before I could say another word, he pulled out another packet from his pocket and waved it.

When I recognized wet wipes from a fast-food restaurant, I was too embarrassed to apologize. Instead, I skulked away, seeking refuge in the farthest corner of the room.

That night you became part of the Hollywood casting call for a neurotic, paranoid, man-basher, extraordinaire, Ms. Freud smiled.

CHAPTER FORTY

I also became aware that it was becoming increasingly difficult for me to trust. I retreated deeper and deeper into myself. I rarely raised the window shades for fear that someone would see inside.

One evening I was startled by a loud rapping on the door. Not expecting anyone. I called out: "Who's there?"

No reply.

I called out again—only louder

Still no reply.

My heart raced as I peaked behind the window shade. I could not see anyone. I remembered my landlord John was usually home in the evening. Hands trembling, I dialed his number.

"John! Someone is at my door. I can't see who's there and they won't answer me!"

"Calm down, Lee," he responded in a soothing voice.

Despite John's attempt to placate me, panic was setting in. I took slow breaths before continuing.

"John—please. I don't want you to confront anyone. Just take a look and let me know if anyone's out there."

A minute or two passed before I heard John's voice call out.

"Hey—what are you doing there? What do you want?"

Trying to see, I pulled the shade up a few inches. I was still unable to see anyone, and so I reasoned the intruder must be standing directly in front of the door.

Again I heard knocking, accompanied by John's voice. "Lee, it's all right to open the door. The man says you know him and he has something to give you."

I cautiously opened the door—to find Bob standing before me holding a plastic bag.

I assured John I did indeed know this person. He nodded and walked away, leaving me to face Bob alone.

I stupidly asked Bob why he didn't answer when I called out. His reply was equally ridiculous. "I didn't know that was you."

Bob held out the plastic bag; it contained an envelope addressed to me. I grabbed the bag—mumbled "thanks," and slammed the door. When I thought about why Bob dragged his ass all the way over to my apartment to deliver a piece of mail, I was certain he expected me to invite him in.

At least you didn't tell him—dream on, said Ms. Freud.

The continuing Bob episodes were balanced by the anticipation created when I checked with the Board of Education for my new payroll number—and I could barely contain excitement when the news finally came. After jumping up and down and screaming, I put a memo containing the coveted information into my principal Fern's mailbox. The next day she paged me.

The moment you've been waiting for, Ms. Freud said—hard work and sacrifice about to be rewarded.

Fern motioned for me to sit at the conference table. This was the first intimate moment I had shared with this no-nonsense, professional lady whom I respected and admired.

Because of the nature of our highly specialized program Fern had more than one educational site under her jurisdiction. I had always assumed I would continue working at my present location, close to home, where I was familiar with students and staff.

Fern instead proposed placement at a site a considerable distance away. When I asked about a position at the main building she explained why that was not possible. She believed a paraprofessional could not make a successful transition where that same person was already employed.

I disagreed.

Fern repeated the offer—and my response was carefully guarded.

"Will my answer seal my fate?"

"No, your answer won't seal your fate," she angrily replied. "But it's possible you will have a long wait before another position becomes available."

Fern's angry response sounded more like a threat than a point of information. "I am completely confused," she continued. "I thought this is what you were working toward. I just don't get it. What's with you?"

The entire time we talked my hands rested on top of the table, palm-side down. Suddenly an "Ah-hah" moment crossed Fern's face. She grabbed my hands in hers.

"No rings," she observed.

"No rings," I agreed.

"What happened?" sshe asked, voice filled with compassion. "When I met you with your husband you both looked so happy."

I explained that my marriage was never what it appeared to be, and that I was just beginning to make decisions for myself.

Fern understood completely. She was an expert of sorts, not because of the Ph.D. after her name, but because she was also a veteran of the marriage wars.

Our meeting ended with a hug and her promise to look into another possible placement.

CHAPTER FORTY ONE

Bea invited me for the first night of Rosh Hashanah, the holiday that marks the beginning of the Jewish New Year. Not wanting to miss a fabulous home-cooked meal, I accepted.

And after I spoke to Bea I had a vivid dream:

I could not decide what to do about a mattress infested with white aphids. Bob was downstairs at a gathering in our old house, which I owned. After the guests left I realized Bob had been lying on the infested mattress which didn't surprise me. Most of the bugs were killed under the weight of Bob's body, but I was concerned that he was transporting them back to his house.

At the holiday meal, I was greeted warmly by Bea and the other guests. Bob was unusually quiet and kept his distance. Everybody knew we were separated and thankfully no one broached the subject. I was congratulated on my graduation and everyone was anxious to learn when I would have my own classroom.

Bea flitted back and forth between the dining room and the kitchen in her bright yellow apron; a honeybee gathering nectar— as usual, too busy to stop even for a moment—until all tasks were completed.

After Bob and I helped clear the table he suggested we go out on the back porch. Once there, he revealed that he was seeing Dr. Adler on an as-needed basis.

Sure, you weren't there to create conflict, observed Ms. Freud, but you thought it sounded like Band-aid therapy.

He was also dating, but continued to imply we could get back together. The conversation concluded with Bob suggesting I call him sometime.

I left with a heavy heart, knowing I had spent an entire evening with a family I dearly loved.

And loved you in return, said Ms. Freud.

It was difficult losing another family. I had already lost one through my previous divorce.

My ex-sister-in-law Jackie called to wish me "Happy Holiday." I always liked Jackie. She was very much like me, funny and intelligent, with an edgy demeanor that implied she was a force with which to be reckoned.

We ended up speaking for at least an hour, sharing many intimate thoughts, and comparing marriage similarities. Not unlike Bob, Allan would not accept blame for what went wrong in that marriage. Much of the time he was either self-pitying or depressed, she said.

"Why did Bea whitewash Bob's past," I asked? "What if we had children together?"

"She never really lied, she just omitted information," Jackie replied. "You have to keep in mind, when Bob was diagnosed there was a stigma attached to mental illness."

"I suppose you're right and it's possible he was misdiagnosed."

My suggestion got a rise out of Jackie. "What do you mean misdiagnosed? His scrambled thinking—his delusions were misdiagnosed?" She shook her head. "Crazy is crazy."

"According to the journal articles I've been reading, years ago psychosis was more often linked to schizophrenia," I replied. "Millions of people in America are suffering with a variety of disorders that may disguise illnesses such as bipolar disorder. One thing I can attest to is that sexual compulsion can be a symptom of bipolar disorder and that's Bob big-time. I suppose it is possible he never received the correct diagnosis."

Jackie wasn't having any of it. "Like I said Lee, crazy is crazy."

The conversation served as confirmation that my marriage was in fact hopeless and that I had made the right decision moving out. I also felt more compassion toward Bea. Who would blame her for wanting to dispose of damaged goods? She saw me as the golden opportunity to unload her 34-year-old, mentally ill, bachelor son.

And then I remembered a story Bob once told me about a three-legged chest of drawers. Instead of discarding the worthless piece of furniture Bea instructed him to cut off the remaining legs. Abracadabra-presto-change-o, the remodeled chest was resurrected and sold to an unsuspecting customer. Each time Bob recounted the event he appeared proud to have been involved in such clever chicanery.

The legs don't fall far from the chest of drawers, do they, sighed Ms. Freud.

Later, principal Fern did in fact understand my reluctance to leap into the abyss. She came through as promised when a position became available where I was already acquainted with some of the staff. Fern patiently explained that although this work site was further away, she was certain I would enjoy working there. She suggested I check out the school the following morning and report back.

There was a lot weighing on this decision. For years I had been riding the merry-go-round from hell. Now somebody was offering me the brass ring and all I had to do was reach out and grab it. This opportunity was the key to my future—to my freedom.

And you were afraid of what, asked Ms. Freud?

That was the last thing I remember thinking before being awakened by the alarm clock's incessant buzzing.

CHAPTER FORTY TWO

As Fern had requested I visited the proposed new work site the next day. And after a fast-paced drive from one end of Brooklyn to the other, I was relieved to find a parking space outside the school entrance. A jovial security guard directed me to the administrative office.

I was introduced to staff members as each clocked in. Everyone encouraged me to consider working at this site. By the end of this brief visit I was impressed with the sincerity and knew I had found a new home—and a new family.

I couldn't wait to tell Fern, "I accept! I accept! I accept! Thank you for not giving up on me."

Later that week, I stood in my classroom unpacking my graduation gifts, revering each one as if it were a priceless antique. And I beamed proudly as I wrote my name on the chalkboard—followed by "teacher."

By the end of my first day I was on cloud nine. On the way home I was bubbling over with excitement. I stopped at Bea's house, hoping she would share the joy. After she congratulated me on my new position, she blurted out, "Bob isn't working—he's not himself. He's depressed all the time, he can't sleep and he spends most of the time in his bathrobe." Bea paused to catch her breath.

"Have you suggested he go back to the psychiatrist for medication? Have you spoken to him about that?"

"Of course, I've tried every way I know to convince him. I've bribed him. I've threatened him. I pointed out that half the people

I know are on Prozac. He promises to do something, but then he doesn't follow through." Bea finally broke down in tears, her body wracked with emotion.

I could not imagine what it was like to raise a mentally ill child. In a feeble attempt to comfort Bea, I put my arm around her trembling shoulders. She gazed up at me, as if seeking absolution. In a voice filled with desperation, she pleaded, "What can I do? What should I do?"

If you had that answer, said Ms. Freud, you would be Freud and Houdini rolled into one—and still together with Bob.

Bea struggled with her next words. This gregarious, effervescent, woman whom I always believed lived in denial had clearly lost her resolve. She was ready to face the reality about her boy.

"Do you think Bob should be hospitalized—just for a short while, until he is stabilized?"

I was startled by her question.

"Shock treatments would help him-they worked before," she continued.

My mind reeled.

"We need two signatures," Bea continued. "Dr. Adler's and the psychiatrist he referred Bob to—I forget his name, I'm sure they would sign the commitment papers."

I found myself unable or unwilling to respond. All I could think of were the possible repercussions from being responsible for Bob's hospitalization.

1. Retaliation after he was released.

2. What would I say to our friends?

3. My family?

4. The world at large?

It would be difficult to acknowledge that I had married a certifiable crazy person. My greatest fear was that I would end up financially responsible for us both. There was no end to the fears that rendered me speechless.

Bea must have surmised that my long silence involved finances. Money was her ultimate solution for solving problems. It was as if she read my mind when she offered to pay for expenses not covered by insurance.

I did not want to be responsible for making the final decision before speaking with Dr. Adler—and I suggested she do the same. I think Bea was grateful Bob was granted a reprieve—even if it was only temporary. I set up an appointment with Dr. Adler for the end of the week.

I should have known when I called my friend Ann she would chastise me for my involvement with Bob and his family. It was difficult for her to understand why I couldn't sever my relationship. How could I explain? Bob was similar to a handicapped child. Even if it was doubtful he would ever change, his loved ones remained hopeful.

Codependency is a bitch, isn't it, said Ms. Freud?

By the time Bea called Dr. Adler, Bob had already experienced a spontaneous recovery. Dr. Adler questioned whether Bea depicted Bob accurately or if she had a flare for melodrama. We agreed that either or both were possible.

With the crisis resolved we moved on to the proper time to divorce Bob. There was no right time. Dr. Adler would support me when I felt the time was right. I planned to wait until I completed my master's degree before filing. I would have a clear mind and I would no longer be burdened with college expenses. I shed a few tears at the realization that this stage of my sad, sad, life was coming to an end.

During the next phone conversation with Bob he acknowledged how terribly he behaved before we split-up and how much he missed being part of a family.

But that conciliatory expression of remorse didn't last long, did it, said Ms. Freud?

Bob went on to complain about how difficult it was to handle everything himself.

Really, sighed Ms. Freud.

But before I could respond, the mood monster roared. Bob accused me of being more concerned about everyone's reaction than with helping him through his illness. He berated me for not getting the signatures needed to commit him to a hospital; he didn't remember I had offered him information for being evaluated as an in-patient. He would always need a scapegoat to blame for his distorted perceptions. Everything that went wrong in his life would continue to be someone else's fault.

But it's also true that his accusation was at least in part true, said Ms. Freud.

I was concerned what people would think if I were divorced twice.

And I was really worried about how my daughter would perceive me if one day I announced, "Sorry honey, I made a mistake—mommy's on the move again. What I thought was the 'knight' who had come to rescue us was only an illusion."

CHAPTER FORTY THREE

But when I began to talk openly about what was happening in my life I became aware of a world filled with people who had been married and divorced—often more than once, and for a variety of reasons.

A talk show's topic on one particular day was, "Until death do us part." The guest psychiatrist explored how mood swings affected other family members, the latest medications and a spouse's role during these difficult times.

Pros and cons about remaining in the relationship were discussed. The psychiatrist went on to explain that it wasn't easy to walk away from the person you loved, especially when children were involved. If there were intermittent periods of acceptable behavior, the tendency was to continue making excuses for the mentally ill person. After watching the show I felt comfortable with my decision to divorce Bob.

I was looking forward to dinner with Michelle and Eric. Michelle was busy cooking while Eric assisted. They looked so cute working in tandem, occasionally stopping for a peck on the cheek or a pat on the butt.

Ah, young love, sighed Ms. Freud.

I thought about quality of life and how the definition varied from person to person. I believed it was about the warmth of the sun, flowers in bloom, passing through the garden gate to my sanctuary, watching my daughter prepare dinner for me and enjoying my son-in-law's homemade chocolate-chip cookies for dessert.

Bob was missing out on so much. He lost everything that mattered.

CHAPTER FORTY FOUR

Graduate school loomed.

In order to secure a teaching position the Board of Education required completion of a master's degree within five years after appointment to that teaching position. And by really pushing myself, I hoped to earn the masters degree in three years.

The first time I laid eyes on Professor Drucker she struck me as a cross between Marlene Dietrich and a dominatrix. Circling the room like a lioness stalking her prey, she conducted lectures perched atop her desk—revealing long, shapely legs which she crossed and uncrossed to the point of distraction.

Students speculated about her age and whether her attire was appropriate—she had a penchant for short leather skirts.

But your opinion never wavered, said Ms. Freud. No matter the age, if you've got it, flaunt it.

The lilt in her voice suggesting she had emigrated from the Caribbean, another professor projected a more subdued and subtle style—that is until a student answered a Professor Simon question incorrectly. In a booming voice that reverberated off the walls, she would address the errant student by last name, resulting in the entire class snapping to attention.

I met Kim in a graduate course. Since we lived in the same neighborhood we decided to take turns driving to evening classes —and in doing so were surprised to learn we shared a similar goal— hoping to acquire a Ph.D.

Without attending college until the age of Social Security eligibility, said Ms. Freud.

But conversation with Kim also made me realize that my world view was very different from hers. My philosophy was: "expect little and you will never be disappointed." One night Kim handed me a bookmark emblazoned with the quotation, "Make Wishes!" When I told her I never did, she replied, sternly, "Start now!"

Teaching opened my eyes to a world I didn't know existed even though I had been working as a teaching assistant. Besides school politics, regulations and deadlines, I had to learn multi-tasking, and the artistic talent I had sublimated while in search of more serious pursuits also resurfaced and I became reacquainted with my creative side.

Madelyn mentored new teachers in our program. The first time she entered my classroom I confessed that I told her I found it difficult to choose goals and objectives for the mentally and physically challenged students. When Madelyn suggested I view each child through a frame which I should form using my thumbs and index fingers I thought she was joking. But as I held up my frame, I was able to recognize subtle movements and facial expressions that had escaped me earlier. I in turn immersed myself in the challenge of becoming the best teacher I could become.

However, the pressure from work and college was getting to me. The endless assignments and schedule changes boggled my mind. This was not education—it was a three-ring circus. I was unable to complete assignments in the time allotted. Student Individualized Education Plans and two college papers were overdue. I dreaded having to ask for an extension to complete student reports—and if I received an incomplete for a course, I would have to repeat the course the following term.

Hopefully with a different professor, remarked Ms. Freud.

When I was under this much pressure I also found it difficult to control anger.

And I missed having a relationship. I knew it meant I would have to put on my happy face and begin hunting in earnest. However that dreaded process only served to fuel anger further. My mind drifted to the possibility of becoming a bag lady, chucking it all and living under a palm tree in Florida. I even thought if I died all my problems would be over.

And feeling sorry for yourself also made you that much more vulnerable, said Ms. Freud.

When Bob begged me to "please" meet him for breakfast, I therefore agreed. I was shocked by his haggard appearance—the dark circles under his eyes reminding me of a horror movie zombie. He wasted no time pointing out he was not working and was also off all medication. He then expressed a desire to remain friends.

I asked if he was concerned about obvious changes in his appearance; his demeanor made it clear he was oblivious to his mental and physical deterioration.

But he was clear about one thing: I was to blame; it was my fault because I would not forgive or forget.

Some things never change, sighed Ms. Freud, and he'll never understand how much pain and suffering he's caused.

My parting words may have sounded cruel and insensitive, but each word was truthful. "Think long and hard before you blame somebody else for your predicament."

CHAPTER FORTY FIVE

Eric had to go out of town on business. I jumped at Michelle's invitation to sleep over. Now that she was married and we both worked at demanding jobs there was less opportunity for mother-daughter quality time. We went out for dinner and a movie. In some ways she still resembled a teenager, but I was proud of the wonderful woman I saw emerging.

My assistant principal scheduled an informal classroom observation which resulted in a memo listing do's and don'ts. By the time I had my first parent-teacher conference I felt more relaxed and confident about my classroom performance.

At the same time—and in my overall life—handling everything on my own became frustrating. My car presented an endless source of problems; if it was not overheating it was burning oil, if the power windows worked the door locks acted up. When it appeared all was well, I discovered a leak in one tire. The *piéce de resistance* was when the muffler fell off. I was unaware that I had lost the tailpipe some time earlier. That explained why I felt drowsy when the car idled in stop-and-go traffic.

God bless Uncle VISA, smiled Ms. Freud. A new car won't come soon enough.

Eric and Michelle were hosting Thanksgiving dinner. The guest list read like an advertisement for an epic movie, announcing "a cast of thousands." I was looking forward to a wonderful day and I hoped Bob would not call or drop by unexpectedly.

The night before Thanksgiving I experienced a disturbing dream.

Bob gained a lot of weight. He was puffing nervously on a cigarette stub, oblivious that his fingers were being singed. He had an infection on his cheek that concerned me. He was upset about the open doors in my house which allowed strangers to come and go at will. Although he spoke in a nasty tone and I was put-off by his appearance, we ended up in bed together.

The dream was particularly disturbing because it revealed a truth that I could not deny.

Despite everything, you still wanted him in bed, sighed Ms. Freud.

Thanksgiving dinner was superb, but I found it difficult to identify with the upbeat conversations swirling around me. Everybody sounded so happy. After consuming a great deal of wine I relaxed and participated. While the rest of the guests were absorbed in a televised football game our friend Mark suggested we put on our coats and step out on the terrace for a breath of air.

This was the first time we were together since he helped me move. He was anxious to know what it felt like to be a teacher, but he seemed even more anxious to know if I had heard from Bob. I assured him I enjoyed my new position even though it was a lot of hard work and Bob was just as crazy as ever. I had the feeling Mark needed assurance that I would be able to handle what he was about to reveal.

He confided that Michelle disliked Bob from the very beginning—and not because he was taking her father's place or that he came between me and Michelle, Mark said. Rather that she wanted very much for me to be happy.

But children and dogs do have an uncanny ability to sense when something is wrong, said Ms. Freud.

Michelle had strong negative feelings from day one. It was distressing to learn how she really felt. I thanked Mark, and I quietly hoped Michelle was not too emotionally scarred.

CHAPTER FORTY SIX

Two college friends suggested I join them for a singles weekend. Dana and Jill were fun; I was the serious one.

At first I couldn't imagine why I had been asked—until I realized the hotel room was cheaper split three ways. Never once did I consider that my company was actually enjoyed.

And wouldn't life be so much easier, said Ms. Freud, if you could just shut me up?

I accepted Dana and Jill's offer.

Upon arrival, we learned the resort was on the verge of bankruptcy. As such, what greeted us was nothing like what I expected.

The buildings were in various stages of decay and so were the guests. There were few activities of interest to singles and the dance music would have appealed to my mother's generation. The whole scene was reminiscent of a convention for losers—and if it were not for my roommates shenanigans the weekend would have been a disaster.

Dana and Jill carried on like teenagers, dancing around our room waiving incense in an attempt to disguise the pungent aroma each was certain wafted into the hallway. When I reprimanded them, both laughed and called me "Mother Hen."

I wasn't concerned what other guests would think; my job was at stake. I was concerned about the notoriety when we appeared in the headlines: "New York Teachers Arrested For Smoking Pot in

Upstate Hotel" But the entire weekend was not all that bad; we did have fun swapping hilarious singles stories.

December is my favorite month. I love the decorations and festivities and I looked forward now to wrapping gifts by myself. Bob would always obsess about how to fold the wrapping paper and insist he place his finger to secure every bow I tied. If the finger slipped we would have to begin again. I felt sorry that Bob was alone for the holidays, but not enough to buy him a present.

Mommy can handle that, Ms. Freud murmured.

My brother insisted I spend Christmas with him. He would not take "no" for an answer and mailed me an airline ticket to Jacksonville. I had a list of things to attend to before I could leave. I had to put up holiday decorations, address greeting cards, purchase gifts, look for a dress for a holiday party, complete a term paper and get together with Michelle and Eric. After that I would relax and enjoy the visit with my brother.

But I decided to celebrate the beginning of the holiday season by attending a dance. Weather and holiday preparation kept the attendance low making it difficult to avoid Bob with such a sparse turnout. When he approached and asked me to dance, he appeared relatively normal.

He likes to dance—you like to dance, so what the hell, reasoned Ms. Freud.

Bob immediately fired questions:

1. What have you been up to?
2. What about Michelle and Eric?
3. Tell me about the kids in your classroom?

And on and on without taking a breath.

His interrogation ended when he expressed how much he resented my independence. When he realized I was not responding he stopped dancing. Before I could pull away he reminded me I could always call to talk.

That night my dream revealed I was at a turning point and was ready to move forward.

I met a woman I had not seen for a long time. She was with her grown son. Their car was in my parking spot and I did not know where my car was. The woman's car had one tire missing. She told me she had used my car earlier and it had fallen apart. I was not angry. My first thought was to call Bob for help. I was not concerned how he would respond. The scene changed to a park-like setting. I was with a group of friends waiting to play volley-ball until everyone disappeared. I carried a book bag filled with magazines for my leisure time and some old clothes. I went into a rundown store and sat next to a sleazy man on a rickety bench. He thought I was an easy pick-up because I sat there for a long time. I was uncertain how long to wait. After one hour I stood to leave. I did not feel obligated to wait any longer. I gathered my possessions and dropped the magazines on the floor. The man started to pick them up, but I stooped down to retrieve them myself. I walked out of the store leaving my old clothes behind.

I spent a delightful Saturday with Michelle. She invited me to see new furniture. Her generation had the right idea—live together for a while and if the marriage works out, then purchase furniture.

During the most recent phone conversation Bea had mentioned to Michelle that Bob would be out of town on business.

Was she kidding, asked Ms. Freud? He's not working. What business? Monkey business?

I envisioned him crying on a prostitute's shoulder while she chastised him for being such a schmuck and lousing up his marriage. After Bob realized what he has sacrificed he calls to tell me he will do anything for us to get back together.

That day dream ended with a snap back to my new life, and moving on.

CHAPTER FORTY SEVEN

It took a great deal of courage for me to respond to a personals ad. Learning Marty had been widowed at the age of 43 tugged at my heart. He changed our meeting place several times and obsessed over how he should dress and the type of food we should eat. Despite my misgivings I agreed to meet him for dinner.

Marty turned out to be a major nut-cake. A nervous little man with thinning, reddish hair and oversized eyeglasses greeted me. He was neatly dressed in "wash and wear" trousers and shirt. His naturally pale complexion was scrubbed to a pinkish glow. He reminded me of a "Cupie" doll.

We talked about how difficult it was to navigate the single's scene.

And then the entrée was served.

Fixating on my baked potato, Marty found it impossible to begin eating.

I preferred to fold back the foil; he insisted the foil be removed completely. Marty continued to stare at my plate while his dinner remained untouched. It was obvious he would not begin his meal as long as the tin foil remained on my potato. Before I could protest, he reached across the table and deftly removed the foil, crumpled it into a ball and placed it on my bread plate.

There was no second date.

The staff Christmas party proved to be enlightening. I would have earned an "A" in my Group Dynamics course if I wrote an essay about the experience. The food and music were fantastic. Everyone knew how to have a good time. By the end of the evening even I danced "doggy" style.

> *Turns out it was all right to let your hair down, said*
> *Ms. Freud, and not be so serious all the time.*

The Christmas visit to my brother was filled with sightseeing, movies and eating—lots of eating. If I had to sum up the week in one word it would have been, "Fun!" I was beginning to enjoy my life and I was trying hard to put Bob out of my mind.

But it wasn't easy when casual acquaintances were anxious to gossip. Many were constantly fishing for salacious busted marriage details, but I only shared that information with close friends.

> *Which didn't stop you from missing Bob, sighed Ms. Freud,*
> *and being upset when hearing about the latest Bob sightings.*

The next time I answered a personals ad proved to be as unsuccessful as the disastrous baked potato attempt. After a series of phone calls and rescheduled meetings, I opted out altogether.

Michelle called to report she and Eric had been unsuccessful in attempts to dodge Bob's dinner invitations. She was reluctant to spend time with him, but Eric insisted it was the right thing to do. When dinner was finally held, Bob advised that it was unlikely we would get back together. He also expressed the hope of not being forgotten.

> *Fat chance of that happening, said Ms. Freud.*

After learning all this from Michelle I had my first anger-filled dream in a long while. When I awoke my fists and jaw were tightly clenched. I had difficulty remembering details, but knew I had dreamed about Bob.

And you were being your own worst enemy, said Ms. Freud.

Instead of dispelling my negative feelings, I rubbed salt in the wounds by re-reading copies of notes Bob and I wrote to each other before separating. One particularly scathing tome captured the demoralizing state of our marriage and the events that led up to saying, "Uncle!"

Dear Bob,

If you feel I am crucifying you then you haven't reached the point in your therapy where you assume responsibility for your actions. I was not the one who screwed around-it was you. The next time you think you are being crucified consider the following:

1. *Sneaking out to see "XXX" rated movies, when you were supposed to be in the college library.*

2. *Supposedly getting lost in Quebec when you went to look at the prostitutes at eleven o'clock at night.*

3. *Carrying condoms "In case you get lucky."*

4. *Finding a cheap earring on the floor of your car and you throwing it out the window without offering an explanation.*

5. *Telling me repeatedly, "None of this is about you. It's about me."*

6. *Dealing with the humiliation of HIV testing.*

This is only a fraction of what I have had to endure. I have been a good and faithful wife, a good mother, a good friend and a good person. Nobody can ever take that away from me. You will never find another woman who is more loving or caring. You aren't being crucified mister...you are just the one being screwed instead of me.

Lee

A friend arranged a blind date for me with a retired college professor. As it turned out he was under the care of a psychiatrist, which was to his credit. At least he was dealing with his problems. He was well-versed on Borderline Personality Disorder and I assumed he was speaking from experience.

I was taken aback when he informed me that most mental health professionals avoided taking on these clients, possibly treating one if the case proved interesting. I wondered if Bob was that "one."

I remembered Dr. Adler explaining how frustrating it was to treat a client diagnosed with Borderline Personality Disorder. There is a disparity between logic and reality. The example he cited was when the client called to report he would be a few minutes late for an appointment. Dr. Adler inquired where he was calling from and explained that the distance precluded his arrival during the appointed time. The client could not understand why Dr. Adler did not have faith in his ability to keep his word.

I needed a diversion to lift me out of the winter doldrums. I signed up for two courses at the "Learning Annex," one dealing with co-dependency and the other with healing the inner child. I hoped each would prove to be a quick fix for the winter blahs.

With a blind date that never materialized, the book I was reading about deviant, sexual behavior—and the dreary weather, I was feeling melancholy.

The desire to see Bob became overwhelming. I finally gave in and called him. I extended an invitation to meet for breakfast with one caveat—that we avoid personal questions.

During breakfast I had to remind Bob about our agreement. When he resumed the conversation without exhibiting anger I mentioned that he appeared calmer and more focused than he had been in a long while. Bob acknowledged that he was taking something and felt much better, but it wasn't long before his demeanor changed and the tension he was experiencing became obvious as he spoke.

I'm not sure what I had expected from our meeting, but I left with the sad satisfaction of knowing Bob would never be 100 percent normal.

You just needed to confirm it for the umpteen-millionth time, said Ms. Freud.

The co-dependency workshop was a boring version of "Can You Top This?" The facilitator introduced herself and recited credentials. Barbara was a licensed psychotherapist, as well as, a published author. Her claim to fame was her self-help books.

My first impression of Barbara was that she fit the stereotype of a co-dependent woman who would endure anything rather than search for a man again. She was a plump, middle-aged woman, with graying, salt-and-pepper hair and a face devoid of make-up, punctuated by bushy eyebrows and heavy jowls. She wore a shapeless, navy blue dress gathered around her ample waist with a vinyl belt which threatened to burst at any moment.

When I gazed around the circle of women sitting on folding chairs I realized there was no one-size-fits-all description of a co-dependent woman. A microcosm of society was present and with one thing in common: being stuck in a relationship and not knowing how to get unstuck.

And you were convincing yourself, said Ms. Freud, that you had already shaken the shit off your shoe and moved on.

Most of the evening was devoted to women whining and Barbara touting books for sale. At the end she distributed business cards and offered a discounted consultation for anyone that mentioned the workshop when calling for an appointment.

Perhaps the end of the month workshop will be more gratifying, said Ms. Freud.

That night I was not surprised when I experienced a brief dream about Bob. He appeared in typical Bob mode—impulsive, inappropriate and predictable.

A week later Bob called to find out if I was still having car problems. We talked for two hours—like when we were first married, before Bob departed for Planet X.

He said he felt ready to begin taking medication seriously—and that his decision had nothing to do with me. He finally understood he needed medication to function. Bob brought up incidents he never discussed before and professed love for me and the kids. He brought up incidents from when he was younger and his brother's battle with depression. He even suggested the possibility there could be a genetic link.

He confirmed that he had not worked in months, but had taken a postal exam hoping to be hired as a mail sorter. He assured me his preoccupation with money, pursuing it, accumulating it and feeling jealous of anyone who had it, would no longer be the driving force in his life. His priorities were creating a structured environment and eliminating stressful situations.

Bob asked if there was a chance we would get back together. He suggested we sell the house, move to Florida and with two salaries we could enjoy a comfortable life.

I said nothing.

Dubious thy name is Bob, said Ms. Freud.

CHAPTER FORTY EIGHT

Whenever I thought I was making progress in separating from Bob emotionally, I was dragged back into the drama by expectations and promises. I envisioned bulls running in Pamploma and red capes frantically waving everywhere I looked. Bob was in desperate need of someone to subsidize him emotionally.

Not me, buddy, said Ms. Freud. Been there, done that.

I congratulated his progress, but said it was unlikely we would recapture what we once had. The conversation ended with Bob promising that in conjunction with therapy he would begin a new regimen of medication with Dr. Perry.

Queried Ms. Freud: And he's going to follow through with that?

I was looking forward to the second workshop. The prospect of exploring one's inner-child appealed to both men and women, with the median age much younger than in the earlier co-dependency workshop.

We were grouped randomly around two large tables. Much of the facilitator's technique was similar to John Bradshaw's teachings. Nevertheless, the content was meaningful and his delivery impressive. After paper and pencils were distributed we were instructed that our grown-up should write a letter to our inner-child.

Dear Inner-Child,

I'm sorry I didn't meet all your needs but I never dealt with my own. Particularly, after my mother sent me to live with my father. I know that's why it took me so long to leave Bob. It wasn't Bob I was leaving…it was my home and my life…all over again. This is not the first time I've lived on my own. It's time to let go emotionally. I can do it. We can do it together.

> *The Grown-Up*

We were then instructed to write a letter from our inner-child to the grown-up.

Dear Grown-Up,

I know you've tried your best to take care of me. You have always taken good care of everyone else. You are a good person. I would say that I forgive you, but there is nothing to forgive.

> *Your Inner Child*

Brave enough to disclose painful secrets, several attendees volunteered to read letters aloud. The rest of the participants sat numbly, some with tears streaming and staining what had been written.

The workshop was tremendously cathartic and you enjoyed it immensely, said Ms. Freud—but you found something wrong.

There didn't seem to be an opportunity for closure—nor any provision for persons with fragile psyches. I knew about exploring feelings, but some persons may have found it difficult to handle such raw emotion.

On the long bus ride home I thought about the house I had left behind. I visualized the cozy bedroom and heard the hum of the ceiling fan as it lulled me to sleep each night. I remembered the artwork I had painstakingly searched for and displayed throughout the house. I was so proud to be the first of our friends to hang pictures in the bathroom.

I had decorated other places in my lifetime, and when there was little money or limited space. Then I had used pictures from calendars, an old cut-up quilt fashioned into curtains for my daughter and furniture bought from her momma's telephone soliciting.

Nothing much had changed. I was still taking care of myself, providing for me, nurturing me. It would be nice to have a man to rely on, but I believed happily ever after was only in fairy tales and completely normal was too much to hope for.

But that didn't stop you from creating a personals ad to run in an imaginary newspaper, said Ms. Freud.

The ad would have read: Just take me for a long ride and a good meal. Yes, I love to travel. Do you like the beach? When do you plan to retire? Are you a good lover? No emotional baggage please, non-smoker a plus.

Later, a newspaper article caught my attention. Coast Guard officials around the world were surprised to discover a 56-year-old woman sailing alone in a 31-foot sailboat. Pat Henry embarked on an eight year voyage after she sold her house during a midlife crisis. At first she intended to live on the boat. Then she thought it would be foolish to sit in the harbor, so she set sail.

What a gal, said Ms. Freud.

I longed for the day when my struggle would be over. There was always unfinished business hanging over me and enduring New York winters was becoming increasingly difficult. Survival hinged on spending every winter vacation in Florida—and that would be costly.

I purchased five lottery tickets. The grand prize was $20 million. I would have settled for $1 million and be gone in a flash.

And you didn't even come close to winning, chided Ms. Freud.

Bea left a message requesting that I call her ASAP.

I was reluctant, afraid I would be sucked into the drama. Feeling obligated got in the way.

"He's a good boy. He means to follow through," Bea pleaded.

"Uh-huh," I said, trying to remain aloof.

"I know he wants to get well…live a normal life."

"Uh-huh."

Bea sounded frantic as she described how Bob refused to make good on his promise for a return to treatment and to get a job.

She was of course hoping you'd jump in, said Ms. Freud.

It broke my heart to tell her I was no longer willing to intercede. I had officially relinquished the caretaker's position. Letting go of Bob was not unlike a death—a death that had already taken place in my heart.

The time had indeed come for me to sacrifice my soul mate in order to survive.

CHAPTER FORTY NINE

As I was leaving for Saturday morning breakfast club I met my neighbor Mel coming out of his apartment.

"Have you seen the take-out ad for pasta in this month's *Pennysaver*?"

"No, I usually throw it out without looking at it."

"Are you kidding me? Wait right here."

Mel bounded up the stairs and emerged with a coupon.

"Buy one, get one free!" he said excitedly. "You choose the pasta and sauce and they give you two bags of garlic rolls—all for less than $6."

"Certainly sounds good to me."

I reached for the coupon, but Mel pulled it back.

"That's not the best part."

I glanced at my watch. I didn't want to be late for breakfast, but neither did I want to appear rude.

"All right Mel, what's the best part?" I inquired, trying not to sound impatient.

"The portions are so big you can split them in half so you have four meals."

Now Mel had my attention. My mouth watered as I imagined tasty meals that would fit into my budget and I would not have to prepare. I thanked him and snatched the coupon out of his hand before rushing off to quiet my growling stomach.

But when I arrived at the diner the gals were more concerned with comparing notes on experiences visiting a psychic than with breakfast. I was told that psychic Bella was the real deal and that I should give her a try. I was skeptical but eventually curiosity led to making an appointment.

I found the experience entertaining, but Bella's revelations were vague, generic, BS. She predicted I would not have a very exciting life and marriage was not in my future. I would never have a lot of money, but I would be comfortable financially and work a few years past retirement age. Bella assured me a long, healthy life and I would live to be 90.

And despite thinking it was BS, you were thankful her predictions did not include Bob, said Ms. Freud.

It was time to cancel out my incomplete course from the previous term. Everyone in class needed psychological statistics to graduate and had saved the dreaded subject for last. I had one step up on the rest; the jargon would not sound cryptic my second time around. The instructor was someone I admired and respected and was preferable to the snippy little creep who taught the class the previous term. I was confident I would succeed this time.

I thought Bob's cousin Carl was just trying to be nice when he insisted I meet him for coffee. When we were face-to-face I realized he felt guilty about not speaking up sooner—and what I learned about his family made my jaw-drop.

Carl was shocked to learn that nobody in the family told me Bob had been diagnosed with schizophrenia prior to our getting married. He found it hard to believe Bob was not on medication all these years. Carl related incidents going back to when Bob was eight years old. He acted out because he was jealous of the attention Bea gave his father and baby brother. On one occasion he became so enraged he cut up the houseplants Bea had nurtured for years, Carl said.

Other family members had been clinically depressed at one time or another, Carl said, but the most shocking bit of information left me speechless.

Bob's grandfather died in a mental institution.

At first the old man appeared to be harmless, spending his days wandering throughout the neighborhood carrying an empty suitcase. When anyone asked where he was going he replied, "On vacation."

Since he didn't bother anyone and never wandered too far, the family left him unattended until mealtime. After bringing him home for a meal, he was returned to the street for the remainder of the day. As he aged, however, his behavior became more erratic until it became necessary to place him in a safe environment until his death.

Carl and I promised to keep in touch. By the time I returned to my car my breathing was so rapid I hyper-ventilated.

Why were you so blind, queried Ms. Freud? How did you not realize what you been dealing with? Your damn relationship was doomed from the beginning.

For years I had negotiated stormy seas in a leaky vessel without a compass.

Why didn't anyone ever tell you the truth before, demanded Ms. Freud?

I had to stop beating myself up. I did not know Bob was damaged goods. This was not like the three-legged chest where I would redesign the furniture by cutting off the remaining legs. I thought about confronting Bea but I was in no mood to hear either her confirmation or denial of the allegations.

A short time later I met with another of Bob's cousins. I could not imagine what tales remained untold. I thought I had already heard everything about Bob and his family.

Boy were you mistaken, said Ms. Freud.

When I met Irene for lunch, she reiterated what Carl had already told me and asked if I knew Bob had once been arrested? I listened in disbelief as yet another family secret was revealed.

"Bob once attempted to assault a bank teller," she began. "Apparently he was dissatisfied with the service he was receiving."

Hanging on Irene's every word, I sat there stunned.

"Well anyway," she continued, "he picked up a chair and tried to smash the glass on the teller's cage. The police were called and Bob was taken to the local precinct."

"You're kidding!" I exclaimed.

Irene went on to explain that Bea showed up with Bob's psychiatrist, Dr. Oliver. She promised to pay for the damage and to keep a closer eye on him. When Dr. Oliver explained Bob was under his care, the bank official agreed not to press charges providing Bob never step foot in the bank again. Bob was released in Bea's custody.

My college drama department produced a farce set in a mental institution. I hoped it would provide some comic relief. I considered inviting a friend until I remembered several were struggling with personal or a family member's emotional problems.

Maybe you're just a mental case magnet, offered Ms. Freud. Or maybe it's like that professor said that everyone is "itsy bitsy schitzy."

I received an anonymous phone call from a member of an organization to which Bob and I belonged. The woman was brimming over with gossip; Bob was on the board of directors and seriously dating one of the other members.

I assured the caller I was not in the least bit interested.

"Please...please," I said aloud, after hanging up the phone. "Someone please take him so I can move on with my life. Let him be someone else's burden."

After I calmed down I wondered if that was what I really wanted. Each time I reconsidered the question, the answer was unequivocally, "Yes!"

My friend Arlene followed-up with her Bob sighting. She had spotted him with a woman and he looked horrible. I told her I wished someone would take him off my hands. Lord knows I was trying every way I knew how to find me a "someone" too.

I crept to places I never dreamed I would frequent, answered personals and asserted myself in ways I didn't know I was capable of. Short of hanging a sign around my neck, I was doing everything I could to find a significant other.

A male friend remarked, "If I were a couple of years younger I would date you." Between that, the Bob sightings, the car alarm going off in the middle of the night and the sexist attitude when I brought the car to the service station, I went ballistic, letting my frustration out on the attendant. Every time the car alarm went off, I reacted like Pavlov's dog and responded with renewed anger.

After the service manager convinced me to leave the car for him to analyze the electrical system, he offered to drive me to work and pick me up later in the afternoon. I apologized for my outburst and accepted his offer. It felt good to have a man take charge.

During our short drive I learned that Ozzie was born in Turkey and worked at the service station part-time when not attending engineering classes at Cooper Union. And when he asked me to dinner his sincerity and swarthy good looks caught me off guard. Remembering my old friend Dr. Feinstein's lecture, I followed his advice to "loosen up" and accepted this invitation from the dark and mysterious young man.

The inviting smile didn't hurt, said Ms. Freud.

Seated in the waterfront restaurant overlooking the Manhattan skyline, I could not help thinking, *he is so damn young*. It almost felt like I was cheating on Bob and robbing the cradle at the same time.

When we were sufficiently mellowed by the wine consumed with dinner, Ozzie suggested we walk along the Promenade. I could feel him trembling each time we stopped to share a kiss. I was certain it was not because of the crisp night air. And at midnight, just like Cinderella, he announced that he had an enjoyable evening but needed to get up early the next day.

That delightfully romantic interlude with young blood did a great deal for your ego, smiled Ms. Freud

The afterglow that followed my date with Ozzie prompted me to think about Leo and how good I felt after seeing him at my graduation party. When I mustered the courage to call, he apologized for not keeping in touch. He had been dealing with family health issues.

Leo promised we would get together for dinner, but when I hung up I knew he was only saying what he thought I needed to hear. I would have to console myself with remembering how Leo's voice sounded when he called me "sweetie," and our final kiss.

CHAPTER FIFTY

February had been particularly beastly with hazardous driving conditions every day. I finalized plans for President's Week and instead of feeling upbeat I was surprised when my emotions took a nosedive.

> *Was it because Bob was dating and you weren't in a relationship, asked Ms. Freud? Or was it that he knew you were leaving for vacation and had not called to ask if you needed a ride to the Amtrak station?*

Even though Michelle had instructed me not to dare let him drive me, I still hoped he would at least make the offer—and focusing on the sun and the palm trees awaiting me in Florida helped me survive the next couple of weeks.

Whenever I traveled by train I had to defend my decision to anyone who inquired why I would want to spend 24 hours in a confined space when I could fly to my destination in a few hours. It was difficult to explain how much I enjoyed the solitude and the feeling of being suspended in a vacuum, where I would leave my troubles behind.

On the way to Florida I reminisced about the nightmarish trip to New Orleans. In retrospect, Bob and I had no business leaving on a vacation. He belonged in a mental hospital and I should have been out of there, but I needed to hold on a while longer. I did not know I was capable of surviving without him. As demented and abusive as Bob was, I stayed long after the ball was over rather than face an uncertain future alone.

During the return trip I had new issues to ponder. Why did my father continue in his miserable marriage to my step-mother?

Was it a form of self-flagellation-punishment for his adulterous relationship that destroyed our family, wondered Ms. Freud?

When I was 12 my parents entered into an acrimonious divorce. My mother never recovered from my father's infidelity and reared two children as a single parent. She resented the close relationship my dad and I shared and her attempts to destroy our bond failed miserably. My dad was always the intermediary, protecting and comforting me—my soft place to fall in the *sturm* and *drang* that was my childhood. He eventually married the "tomato" he had been screwing around with and spent the rest of his life atoning for his indiscretion

I returned from vacation in the midst of a New York City snowstorm. As much as I detested the cold, I had to admit the sight of falling snow made me happy to be alive. I was lucky to find a line of taxicabs waiting for fares. The ride home took an exceptionally long time and while the meter clicked mercilessly I ran short of money. The driver insisted I leave a suitcase for collateral while I went inside for a checkbook.

Once back and settled in, I retrieved messages and heard a very disturbing one from a friend who had been previously diagnosed as manic-depressive.

Jan had been desperate to reach me while I was in Florida. Even though she was taking medication she had experienced a couple of really bad weeks. The message was a reminder of what my life would be like had I remained with Bob. By the time I returned her call Jan's psychiatrist had already adjusted her meds and she was functioning relatively well.

There was also an urgent message from Bob. He ran out of health insurance forms and needed to ask me a question about medical coverage. I became angry as I searched through my employee benefits manual. The knowledge that Bob wouldn't take out life insurance or draw up a will when we were living together only intensified my anger.

Your health insurance is keeping him alive, sighed Ms. Freud, while you barely satisfy your deductible.

I slipped the forms into an envelope and reluctantly dropped them in the mailbox.

My dad called to find out if I arrived home safely. I heard my step-mother's snide remarks in the background. She never let up on my father—always monitoring what he said, always eavesdropping—just like Bob.

My dad screamed at Roberta to shut up. I asked him to please not do that when he was on the phone with me. Listening to them fighting reminded me of my own dysfunctional marriage. My father's excuse for staying in his relationship was, "You should have told me to leave long ago."

I reminded him of all the times I had listened to his feeble excuses for staying, and then counseled him, promising to carry him out piggy-back, if necessary. He had to make up his own mind; it was not my job to make the decision for him. I had enough crap going on in my life and I did not do crazy anymore.

When I hung up I realized I had dumped on my dad. He really didn't deserve it. I felt better after I wrote a letter apologizing for sounding unsympathetic.

When Bob called to thank me for the insurance forms we talked for over an hour. He was back in therapy. He regretted past behavior and acknowledged I had been a good person and a good wife.

And he sounded pathetic, Ms. Freud said, when he confessed that he was jealous because you are doing something meaningful with your life and he was stagnating.

I wondered if he was biding his time until Bea died, waiting to live off his inheritance. From Bob's appearance the last time I saw him it was conceivable she could outlive him. He smelled from far too many cigarettes, and was thinner than ever before. It was obvious Bob was experiencing some difficulty with his hair, either placing it or finding it. I felt sorry for him until he opened his mouth to make a snide remark.

You never had to wait long before being reminded why you were separated, said Ms. Freud.

I was still hoping for a meaningful relationship with somebody new, but I did not see how I would possibly fit another human being into my schedule. I was tired of work and school, dating jerks and weirdoes—and being bundled up but still freezing.

I awoke at five in the morning with a million thoughts. I held Teddy's paw hoping to fall back to sleep. When the alarm clock rang an hour later, I was in a foul mood and should have called in sick.

The snowdrifts prevented school buses from picking up many disabled students. Attendance was low and dismissal was ten minutes away when the assistant principal suddenly appeared at my classroom door. From her displeased expression I knew I was about to be reprimanded. Jean expected me in her office before I departed.

She wanted to know what was going on or not going on when she entered my classroom. I explained that we were ready for dismissal when she entered. At the same time I realized that it must have looked as if I had not done anything all day.

You work hard and devote yourself to the students, said Ms. Freud. But how could she know that teaching special needs children filled the hole in my soul?

She assured me that she knew I was a capable teacher.

She made suggestions on how to engage students at the end of the day, i.e., review a list of accomplishments or discuss plans for the following day, just as long as we are engaged in an activity.

We set up an appointment for an official observation. I envisioned sleepless nights in an effort to develop the perfect lesson plan, covering all content areas and modifying it for each student's varying exceptionalities.

During the drive home I was consumed by intense anger that was impossible to shake. I fantasized Bob died, and for the first time I felt completely disconnected from him.

One of my breakfast club friends arranged a blind date for me with her neighbor. Burt was a widower who lived in a magnificent house on the bay and owned a lucrative auto repair business. Sounded good to me, but of course there was a hitch. His 30-year-old son lived at home. Burt described the young man as "troubled" and went on to explain when his wife was alive she dealt with those problems. That didn't include getting him professional help, Burt said, and now he was left to deal with the mess alone.

The weather bureau warned of a snow shower the evening Burt and I planned to go out. The forecast predicted a late night arrival. Burt suggested a neighborhood restaurant and promised to monitor the weather during dinner. We were engrossed in conversation, unaware that a heavy snowfall had begun to blanket the city. When Burt questioned our waiter about the latest weather report we learned the snowfall was heavier than first predicted.

I was concerned about the licensing exam scheduled for the following morning and I was certain it wouldn't be cancelled. I even wondered aloud how I would get downtown the next day. Burt suggested I pack whatever I needed and he would drop me off at my daughter's house. Michelle lived close to the testing site and owned a four-wheel drive vehicle. With everyone pitching in I was sure I'd make it to the test site.

Burt called. He sounded pleased I had aced the exam, but he never called again. It was just as well. He seemed overwhelmed with his newfound responsibility. His situation also presented problems and I had enough of my own.

There was never a dull moment. I was certain I was experiencing some sort of endurance test. I arrived home to find half the bathroom ceiling ripped out. I had left the key with Mel to let in the plumber. We were still trying to locate the source of the upstairs leak.

And the open ceiling had revealed another problem.

Termites!

I insisted the landlord send an exterminator immediately. Thinking about how Bob would have reacted under similar circumstances found me caressing a cynical smile.

Lucky for me, I had prepared materials for my official observation the previous day. On the way to work the car overheated. I ran a number of red lights on the way to a service station closest to work.

I called Jean and explained that I would be late. She sounded sympathetic and suggested we reschedule the observation for another day. No way would I survive another day. I took a cab the rest of the way and arrived in time.

And were thrilled when you received a satisfactory rating, said Ms. Freud.

A letter arrived from my dad in response to the long, emotional letter I had written after our last phone conversation. It was a relief to know he understood what I was going through and he promised to be more sensitive in the future. I was fortunate to be getting closer to my dad. I was sorry I never had the same opportunity with my mother.

Bob called to find out if I had received his reimbursement check from my insurance company. He was being treated with Lithium and had resumed therapy. He regretted not having done so sooner.

Locking the barn after the horse has run off, queried Ms. Freud?

I wished him well, but I did not believe for a moment that he would adhere to the regimen.

I rarely cooked. With my schedule it did not make sense to bother for just one person. Thinking about it made me chuckle. I remembered an old joke about the person who after entering the pearly gates was served tea and toast. Although it was late in the day, he couldn't help notice that "down below" everyone was enjoying a sumptuous meal.

The next day it was the same—tea and toast while he observed the fabulous feast served below. Finally he asked St. Peter, "Why am I served such a sparse meal while those sinners are fed so well?" Shrugging, St. Peter replied, "It doesn't pay to cook for two people."

I invited Michelle, Eric and a friend from work for dinner. I prayed there would not be a termite outbreak but I forgot to say a prayer for the plumbing. In the midst of washing dishes the toilet began to gurgle. I used the plunger until the ejector pump kicked in and cleared the sewer line.

People were falling apart all around me. I did not understand what was keeping me from doing the same thing. It would have been so easy to just curl up in a corner and withdraw from life. What kept me going?

Where does that strength come from, wondered Ms. Freud?

My single's group chartered a bus for a day of shopping at an outlet mall. Eric was going out of town and Michelle planned to sleep over and join me on the bus trip. She hoped Bob would not be going, but of course he was. He offered Michelle spending money; she declined.

During the trip his booming voice could be heard above all others. Just like his mother he jabbered incessantly, and entertained the captive audience with endless stories—some fact, others fiction.

I learned that Bob was still not working.

And if you had stayed with him, Ms. Freud observed, you would have ended up supporting him because he never would have spent his money.

Michelle and I enjoyed a wonderful day together. On the way home she asked how I tolerated the sound of Bob's voice.

"I used to have a knee-jerk reaction whenever I heard him until I learned to block his voice from my mind," I told her. And listening to him now reinforced for me what I already knew.

He's not normal, never was and never will be, said Ms. Freud.

Getting back together was not an option. I was thankful I left before Bob crashed completely. There was no denying we had both derived something from the marriage. I was the guinea pig in the experiment to find out if Bob could sustain a long-term relationship and he was the patient I envisioned treating when I became a psychotherapist.

Eric and Michelle had been discussing starting a family. When Michelle called to say she was three months pregnant, I was thrilled. I was going to be a grandma.

I thought back to when Bob and I would lie in bed on leisurely Sunday mornings, daydreaming what it would be like to have a toddler bouncing between us after a sleepover. We had looked forward to becoming grandparents someday. I wished that for Bob as much as for myself and knowing the fantasy no longer included him, saddened me.

The life and love we once shared no longer existed. It had been a long and difficult journey for us both. And I had not arrived at a decision before agonizing over a relentless internal dialogue of what ifs:

1. What if Bob's mental state deteriorated and he had to be institutionalized?

2. What if he committed suicide as a result of me filing for divorce?

3. Would I feel responsible?

4. Would I be able to deal with my guilt?

I had no choice, but to persevere. I dreaded having to deal with Bob's histrionics in a courtroom, but the time had come to end our marriage legally.

PART SIX

WATCH YOUR
STEP GETTING OFF

CHAPTER FIFTY ONE

Before hiring a divorce attorney I had heard horror stories about excessive billing, being handed off to a colleague when the original lawyer wasn't available and feeling uncomfortable with male representation. My main concern was that I was the one who walked away from the marriage.

I was referred to delightful young woman. Karen put me at ease the moment I stepped inside her tidy home office. She assured me that under the circumstances, "constructive abandonment" was a legitimate cause for leaving my dangerous situation.

"You're going to hear things that are unbelievable," I warned.

"There is nothing you could say that would shock me or that I haven't heard before."

I took a deep breath before reciting the woeful tale. Karen filled half her yellow pad with notes as I purged myself of toxic emotions kept buried inside for years. I was ready to ride the merry-go-round from hell one last time.

And I wish I would have been there to see the look on Bob's face when he was served with the "Action for Divorce." I'm sure he believed that until the end of time we would remain married while living apart.

Whenever we met with the lawyers Bob attempted to bully everybody, particularly Karen. During the discovery process Bob refused to answer "full disclosure" questions and would not comply with either lawyer's requests to produce pertinent documents.

Without the pertinent information we would not be able to reach an out-of-court settlement. Bob had once accused me of planning to take him to the cleaners.

That was never your intention, said Ms. Freud. You only wanted what you were entitled to under the law.

Before Bob and I separated I was advised to Xerox every statement, bankbook and tax return I could locate. Bob went ballistic when I produced copies of documents he denied existed. Throughout our marriage Bob would freak out if I mentioned his finances. He insisted that was his business and nobody else's.

And when Bob's financial records were finally revealed it became blatantly clear he had manipulated bank accounts, and money had been disappearing for years. Some of it was traced to a KEOUGH account in his name that I never knew existed.

During these meetings my stomach churned when I recalled incidents where Bob physically or psychologically abused me. When those recollections intensified I would have to fight back waves of nausea. Karen often called for a break whenever she sensed my distress. She would put an arm around my shoulder and escort me to the water cooler. After I washed down several antacid tablets, she would offer to reschedule.

"We can stop for the day if you like."

"And give that bastard the satisfaction of knowing he still has this much power over me? No way. Give me a moment until my stomach settles down and I'll be fine."

When we returned to the conference room Bob's lips were usually curled in a self-satisfied smirk.

Which you loathed, Ms. Freud said, and often fantasized about obliterating permanently.

Karen and I discussed the possibility Bob may be involved in business dealings with his brother, but she advised me to forget about following the money trail outside New York. Doing so would be counter-productive and involve hiring a lawyer or private investigator licensed in the other state. The additional expenses would not be worth the outcome.

Karen made it clear, "We're not dealing with Donald Trump here." She was concerned that I may lose my "nest egg" if divorce proceedings dragged on for too long; she advised me to cut losses and move on.

Bob continued to stonewall at every turn. There were days he was uncommunicative, placing two fingers—the sentries guarding his words—across his lip. At other times he insisted on ridiculous stipulations.

At times you didn't care if you wound up penniless, said Ms. Freud. You'd rather go to court than allow him to screw you like he had done throughout the marriage.

It became seemingly impossible to agree on an out-of-court settlement. After the last exhausting and unproductive meeting, intense anger permeated a dream.

When Bob arrived in a security guard's uniform he appeared to have gained back the weight he had lost previously. He smiled broadly and invited me to lunch, but before I could reply I felt his gun in my back. I wasn't frightened when I turned to confront him. In his other hand were the items stolen from our house he claimed were evidence. Bob announced that he was there to arrest me. I called his bluff before I woke up.

I needed a diversion. I decided to attend the annual "Triple Pier" antique and collectible show in Manhattan. I searched for pottery similar to the Satsuma I left behind when I moved out.

Resisting the impulse to reach out and caress it, I could not bring myself to purchase the small, inexpensive vase I passed by several times. Up until that moment I had not realized how much I missed the collection that would no doubt be in dispute during the divorce proceedings.

The gentlemen who leased the booth stepped forward. "I can see you would really like to own this vase," he said in a charming British accent. Before I could respond he reduced the price. When I started to explain that I was not concerned about the money tears welled up and details of my circumstances came tumbling out.

"Nonsense, you shall have it!" he declared. He wrapped the vase in tissue paper and placed it in a small, brown shopping bag.

He pushed aside the money I held out in payment. "Let this symbolize the beginning of your new life," he smiled.

For the rest of the day I carried my treasure as if it were the Hope Diamond.

CHAPTER FIFTY TWO

At every court appearance Bob vacillated between being emotionally disengaged to openly hostile. The proceedings dragged on endlessly and became increasingly unproductive. Whenever we made a small amount of progress Bob became obstinate—two steps forward and one step back.

You fought tooth and nail every step of the way, said Ms. Freud.

Each time Bob refused to cooperate the judge threatened him with contempt-of-court charges, including after Bob's refusal to evenly distribute the extensive collection of Japanese pottery we had accumulated over the years.

When we first met Bob had showed me a tea set wrapped in yellowed newspaper stored in his basement. The tea set matched the ice bucket originally given to my grandparents as a wedding gift.

The judge ordered the collection divided between us.

When Bob vehemently refused to give up any of the Satsuma, I was certain he would spend the night in jail. Instead, the judge warned that if he did not submit a property distribution list by the next court appearance, he would order the entire collection brought to court, unwrapped, appraised, re-wrapped and distributed as per his decision.

And the lawyers would bill the contracted hourly rate, said Ms. Freud, no matter how long the argument lasted.

After Bob realized the judge was serious he promised an amicable decision by the next court appearance—but I should have known when dealing with Bob, a fair and equitable distribution would be difficult, if not impossible.

We argued back and forth on the phone and in person, but finally agreed on how to divide the collection. Bob offered to deliver my pieces. To avoid errors, I believed it made more sense to wrap the items together. To my surprise, Bob did not object.

When I arrived at the house the stench from rotting garbage was unmistakable. The items I agreed to were on the coffee table in neat rows arranged by size. An industrial-sized roll of bubble-wrap took up the entire couch. In silence Bob and I sat on the carpet completing the task of wrapping and packing the Satsuma.

He helped me carry the cartons, placing them in my car's trunk. He made it clear that he wanted to still be a part of Michelle and Eric's life—and wished me well. We shook hands with the understanding that the lawyers would take care of the rest.

During the drive home I reflected on how comfortable I felt sitting on the floor in our house. That was until I remembered that whenever I let my guard down it was only a matter of time before Bob's craziness emerged.

And time then to say goodbye to warm and fuzzy, said Ms. Freud.

Michelle's pregnancy was progressing according to schedule and after her first sonogram she proudly displayed a picture of what appeared to be a very active baby boy. She begged me not to tell Bea or Bob; she was unsure how to handle our complicated situation.

And we were shopping for a baby layette when we saw Bea and Bob headed our way. There was no way to hide Michelle's pregnancy. Bea was her usual effusive self, cooing and patting Michelle's belly while Bob appeared disinterested. Bea made Michelle promise to tell her when the baby is born. She wanted to buy a "nice" present. Bob was silent the entire time. We were relieved he didn't cause an unpleasant scene.

Throughout the divorce fiasco I continued to touch base with Dr. Adler. I hoped he would direct me toward the happy life I was longing for. He helped me understand that he was in fact only a guide.

He shines the light; you walk the path, reminded Ms. Freud.

I often looked to Dr. Adler for permission to make decisions. After all the years with Bob I had forgotten how to set boundaries. When Bob was spinning off in different directions I was always trying to reel him in. After a while it became impossible to set boundaries for either of us.

Dr. Adler had explained that we have to question the belief system we learn in childhood, i.e., being taught to wait an hour after we eat before going swimming. "Was that rule realistic if we consumed a salad instead of a meatball hero?" he asked.

One week into Michelle's ninth month, I received an urgent call from Eric informing me she was in labor. The drive to the hospital was a blur. I took no notice of where I parked. I was consumed by only one thought; my baby was having a baby, three weeks early.

An obstetrical nurse greeted me with the news that Eric was in the delivery room with Michelle and all was well. Her words were of little comfort as I waited alone. Not knowing what was taking place became unbearable. The nurses continued to reassure me and tell me not to worry.

When a nurse entered pushing an Isolette containing a tiny red-faced baby I was overjoyed. He was swaddled in a blanket, wearing a tiny blue knit cap and for a split second, I imagined Michelle's father's face peaking out from under the cap. The similarity was startling.

"It's a boy!" the nurse announced. "Your daughter is fine. You can relax now." I was overcome with emotion when I realized I was a Grandma.

After Harris was born I tried to spend as much time with him as possible. He was a great stress reliever. Whenever dealing with Bob became unbearable, I rushed over to see Harris and love him up until he squealed with delight. Then all would be right with my world again. When I held him I felt that love was boundless. We all have the capacity to love, consecutively, simultaneously, from near or far. All we ask in return is that love be reciprocated.

That's all you ever wanted, said Ms. Freud.

I dreaded each court date for fear Bob would flip out or fail to appear. I worried that if we put the house on the market he would not allow prospective buyers in—or they would be discouraged by his behavior after entering the house.

After investing a great deal of myself into making the house a home, I also found it painful to imagine strangers living in it.

Truth is, said Ms. Freud, you were upset that Bob was warm and cozy, enjoyed decent plumbing, plush carpeting and the absence of termites, while you lived like a mole in a hole.

Bob offered to buy me out, but the house would have to be refinanced. He was displeased with the rates the mortgage companies proposed. He kept flip-flopping between one lender and another until both his lawyer and the judge were ready to tear out hair and I had consumed a truck-load of Pepto Bismol.

After the judge ordered Bob to secure financing before our next court appearance, Karen whispered in my ear, "I don't know how you lived with this man as long as you did."

The next court date had to be postponed. Bob was turned down for refinancing because he once had a $10,000 lien against the house.

Bob's lawyer was trying to move things along by helping him search for a more lenient lender.

My dad called to tell me he would have to postpone his annual visit; his heart was not functioning properly. Fluid was building up in his lungs and his cardiologist wanted to implant a pace-maker.

In the background, Roberta shrieked hysterically. "What am I going to do if something happens to you?" She was concerned how she would survive without her cash cow/chauffer. My dad predicted Roberta would have a boyfriend before his body was in the ground.

I wanted to fly down, but dad assured me the surgery was routine. I was concerned about his health, but I was also disappointed he would miss out on seeing his new grandson. I promised that Michelle and I would bring Harris for a visit when I had time off from work.

Expenses incurred while attending graduate school and divorce lawyer fees were weighing heavily. I considered selling my engagement ring, but it represented the hopes and dreams I had never dared to imagine when I was younger. I had to keep in mind that the ring had nothing to do with Bob's feelings for me.

He used it in the same way a fisherman chooses a lure to attract an unsuspecting fish, said Ms. Freud.

We finally had a closing on the house. When we met with the bank's lawyer, Bob was his usual weird self. He displayed the familiar phony smile and after giving me a big, "Hello!" he thanked me.

"What are you thanking me for, for giving you so many years of my life?"

"No—for coming here today."

I didn't understand what he meant. All I cared about was that we were one step closer to ending this marriage.

CHAPTER FIFTY THREE

My dad decided to move into an assisted living facility. At first I was concerned that he was giving up his will to live. He assured me that was not the case. If anything, it was his desire for a better quality of life that prompted the decision. He could no longer rely on Roberta to administer his medications properly and he looked forward to peace and quiet at this time in his life. But I was still unable to shake the feeling that this was the beginning of the end.

Weeks passed before I heard from Bob. He called to tell me he had received the escrow check from the bank and suggested we meet for breakfast to give me my half of the money. I hoped to conclude our business as quickly as possible, but during the meal there was no mention of money.

After the waitress handed Bob a check for breakfast, he suggested we go somewhere else and continue the conversation. I indicated that I wished to conclude our business then and there.

Bob pulled out the escrow check and thrust it across the table with a pen. When he went into a tirade about how the check really belonged to him and he was not obligated to share, it became clear he had no intention of splitting it.

I accused him of luring me under false pretenses and stood to leave. Only then did he reveal his personal check, payable to me for half of the escrow.

Bob implored me not to leave. "Don't be angry! Don't run away!"

"Why do you do these things?"

"I can't help it; I have to say what's on my mind."

My fury could not be contained. I grabbed the check and tore it up.

"Use my half of the money to buy yourself a present and every time you look at it, think of me and the family you've lost."

Hot tears seared my cheeks as I ran toward my car. I peeled away from the curb, tires squealing, horns blaring.

Foolish, impulsive behavior, said Ms. Freud, but you didn't give a crap.

I expected to feel a sense of loss after the judge granted the divorce. Instead I felt liberated. I was rid of the burden I had carried for so long. I compared divorce to when a loved one dies after a long illness. The grieving process begins long before the final breath.

Bob whispered in his lawyer's ear when we were signing the divorce papers. The lawyer's face flushed with embarrassment as he restated Bob's request. "My client feels Lee should pay for the court reporter and transfer fees." Karen shook her head in disbelief.

"If I am forced to pay one more penny than the costs we agreed upon, I am going to tear up these papers and we can start all over again."

The two lawyers huddled, followed by more whispering between Bob and his lawyer. The request was withdrawn, and on the way to the elevator I thought of my friend Laura's favorite expression: "It is what it is."

I met with Dr. Adler shortly after the divorce papers were signed. He referred to Bob's "craziness" for the first time and assured me I had done everything possible to help him. I expressed the fear that I would never find anyone to fill the void in my life. Dr. Adler insisted that would change, but "It takes time to remove the quills after an encounter with a porcupine."

When the divorce became final, friends celebrated with me. Nobody was happier for me than Sylvia. I kept the promise I made to myself and continued our summer friendship long into the winter.

When I suggested Michelle take my engagement ring her reaction was so intense anyone would have thought I had offered her a live hand-grenade. She did not want anything that would remind her of Bob. She suggested I sell the ring and do something nice for myself.

I vowed to nurture my inner child, reward her for the emotional pain she—we—had endured. I also followed Michelle's advice and sold the ring. On the way home from the jeweler I stopped at a travel agency and inquired about a European vacation.

The next day I visited the furniture store where I had once agonized over a decision to make my first purchase after leaving Bob. This time there was no hesitation, no indecision. I knew what I wanted and I had the money to pay for it. I bought a triple wall unit I knew would take up a large portion of the limited space in my apartment.

But what better way to display the spoils of my battle—the beloved Japanese pottery, said Ms. Freud.

I remained in touch with Bea and Ernie. I learned Bob had discontinued therapy and was off medication. He was unable to work and had applied for Supplemental Social Security.

Michelle, Harris and I flew down to visit my dad. My brother met us at the hotel. The assisted living facility was nicer than I had expected. I was relieved to find an attractive, clean, environment with a friendly, competent staff.

At first my dad appeared frail, but when he spoke his voice sounded strong. He insisted on holding Harris on his lap and proudly posed for snapshots. We spent as much time as possible with him.

And by the end of the visit, Ms. Freud said, you knew this would be the last time together as an extended family.

It was.

CHAPTER FIFTY FOUR

When Michelle and Eric announced another child was on the way, I wondered how Harris would react to a new baby. I wasn't sure how I was going to react. I had already given so much of my love to Harris. Then I remembered what I discovered shortly after he was born, love is boundless.

A friend called to inform me Bob was selling his house and moving in with the gal he used to ogle at the beach club. I wished them no ill will. Everyone deserves to move on. I wondered if she would experience her own merry-go-round ride. I smiled knowing, that part of my life was over.

Every so often I drove past the house where Bob and I had lived and loved.

Before his madness drove you apart, reminded Ms. Freud.

The house was decorated for Christmas. Twinkling lights surrounded the picture window framing a beautifully decorated tree. Instead of continuing toward home I stopped to buy a bottle of wine wrapped in holiday paper.

I wasn't sure what I would say when I handed the gift to the new owners, but my need to make the gesture was compelling. When I rang the doorbell a young woman answered.

For a moment she appeared confused. After all, I was a stranger offering a gift. Her husband joined her in the doorway and I envisioned the happy couple on a holiday greeting card.

I noticed the carpeting had been replaced with wood flooring and the wood paneling Bob hated and I loved, had been removed. Everything looked neat and clean, the way it was when I lived there.

I introduced myself as the ex-wife of the former owner and explained that I was just stopping by to wish them well. The woman smiled broadly and complimented me on the lovely house. She motioned for me to enter and asked if I would like to see the upstairs. I declined her gracious offer and handed her the bottle of wine. When I drove away it was with the knowledge that I would not be compelled to pass that way again.

Appropriately enough, that night I dreamed about Bob.

I was in a nightclub, but I wasn't sure if I appeared in the show or if I was a patron. I was high above the stage. Bob was seated at a table below me. He had to strain his neck to see me. His usual smirk was plastered across his face. Each time he looked at me, I ignored him. When he stood to leave I took a peek at his companion. I was satisfied when I saw she was unattractive.

Baby Rose came into to the world larger and feistier than her brother—another beautiful baby to love. After she came home from the hospital, Harris was delighted when he was allowed to hold his baby sister. He amused everybody by reciting the words he planned to teach his sibling. He was too young to understand it would be some time before Rose would be ready for the tutorial.

A popular talk-show hostess had her viewers writing in a "wish" journal. I never believed in making wishes or in fate. I was so used to making things happen that I didn't leave a window of opportunity for events to occur naturally. I vowed to change gears, slow down and learn new steps in my journey through life.

And in the meantime, reminded Ms. Freud, you'll be content to enjoy family, friends and your two precious grandchildren.

Occasionally I would ask myself, "What do you really want out of life?" At first my answer was, "Someone who is normal," but as time went by I doubted such a person existed.

Everybody is a little weird, said Ms. Freud.

Several years passed before I saw Bob again at Bea's funeral.

When we met afterward, I was shocked by his appearance. He looked gravely ill. He was painfully thin and his skin was ashen.

He looks like death warmed over, said Ms. Freud.

I was not privy to Bob's feelings about the loss of his mother—or about inheriting the money for which he had waited his entire life.

But he will never experience the elusive happiness or fulfillment that he longed for during his lifetime, said Ms. Freud.

A short time later I heard through the grapevine that Bob had succumbed to pancreatic cancer. Nobody deserved such a horrific and untimely end. At first, the news numbed me. But when I realized Bob would be gone forever, my animosity was replaced with overwhelming sadness.

After Dr. Adler expressed his heartfelt condolences, I assured him I was handling Bob's death as well as could be expected.

In all the years we were separated and subsequently divorced, so strong were my feelings about violating his space that I was never able to sleep on Bob's side of what was then no longer even his bed.

He brought a passion to my life that energized and motivated me. I achieved goals I would never have dreamed of had I not been forced to ride the emotional merry-go-round that was an integral part of our relationship.

You never stopped loving Bob, said Ms. Freud.

But I could not ride the merry-go-round forever.

EPILOGUE

Closure has been an important component throughout my life. This need to tie up loose ends prompted me to visit the Memorial Park where Bob is interred.

Standing alone in front of the cold marble wall I experienced a profound sense of loss. A plaque with his name and dates of birth and death mark Bob's final resting place. At any time during his tormented life was he not a loving son or brother?

In death he lies alone; his father, mother and brother are interred elsewhere.

I pray that Bob is free of the demons that dominated his life. Rest peacefully.

In the moments before dawn
A symbol of hope waits over the horizon.
The golden rays herald a new day.
In the shadows the calliope is silent
The merry-go-round...still;
The journey is over.

AUTHOR INFORMATION

Lee B. Ravine holds a Bachelor of Arts in Psychology and a Master of Science in Special Education. She began her career as a paraprofessional with the New York City public school system and went on to teach her beloved special needs students.

After moving to Florida she worked as a substitute teacher and volunteered as a domestic violence victim's advocate with the Palm Beach County Sheriff's Office.

Lee continues her volunteer work as a facilitator with the Center for Group Counseling and is available as a guest speaker.

Despite her busy schedule she manages to find time to work on a novel exposing the closely guarded secrets hidden behind the gates of a country club community.

INVITE ONE OF SOUTH FLORIDA'S TOP SPEAKERS TO YOUR ORGANIZATION.

Lee B. Ravine promises an interesting, informative and entertaining talk on related topics before groups of any size.

For more information call 561-470-1580
or email: ProfLBR@aol.com
www.LeeRavine.com